How to Sell, Then Write Your Nonfiction Book

A Comprehensive Guide to Getting Published—From
Crafting a Proposal to Signing the Contract and More

Blythe Camenson

New York Chicago San Francisco Lisbon London Madrid Mexico City
Milan New Delhi San Juan Seoul Singapore Sydney Toronto

Library of Congress Cataloging-in-Publication Data

Camenson, Blythe.
    How to sell, then write your nonfiction book : a comprehensive guide to getting
published — from crafting a proposal to signing the contract and more / Blythe
Camenson.
        p.   cm.
    ISBN 0-658-02104-4
    1. Authorship—Marketing.   2. Authorship.   I. Title.

PN161.C325   2002
808'.02—dc21   2002020754

*I am pleased to dedicate this book to all the writers
I've worked with over the years.
You've taught me as much as I've taught you—
and for that I will be forever grateful.*

7 8 9 10 11 12 13 14 15 16 17 18 19 20 21 22   EUS/EUS   0 9 8 7 6

ISBN-13: 978-0-658-02104-6
ISBN-10:   0-658-02104-4

Cover design by Nick Panos
Cover photograph copyright © Christoph Hellhake/Stone
Interior design by Rattray Design

Contents

Preface   vii

Acknowledgments   ix

1 The Business of Publishing and How It Affects You   1

Book Categories and Where Your Book Fits In   2

What's Hot, What's Not   4

What Publishers Are Looking For   4

Who's Publishing Nonfiction   6

Frontlists, Midlists, and Backlists   11

Who to Approach   12

Working with an Agent   13

How Literary Agencies Are Structured   17

Location, Location, Location   18

How to Find an Agent   18

2 Finding and Defining Book Ideas That Sell   21

Finding Book Ideas   22

Ten Steps to Judge the Merit of Your Ideas   22

Advice from Publishing Professionals on Selling
    Your Nonfiction Book   25

Identifying Trends and Avoiding Fads   26

Who Can Sell, Then Write a Nonfiction Book?   28

Experts on the Bestseller Lists   29

Making Yourself More Saleable   30
What Can Nonexperts Write About?   31

3 **How to Approach Agents and Editors**   **33**

Can I Really Sell the Book Before I Write It?   34
How an Agent Sells Your Book Idea   36
What Happens Once Your Idea Lands on an Editor's Desk   37
Tools of the Trade   41
Query Letters That Grab Attention   42
The Elements of a Book Proposal   49
Cover Letters   66
Follow-Up Letters   69
Completed Manuscripts   70
Formatting and Submission Details   71
Keeping Track of Your Submissions   74
Can You Resubmit Once Your Idea Has Been Turned Down?   74
Turnoffs   75

4 **Sample Query Letters and Proposals**   **77**

Query Letter and Proposal Sample #1   78
Query Letter and Proposal Sample #2   104
Query Letter and Proposal Sample #3   138

5 **Money and Contracts**   **163**

Advances   164
Agent-Author Contracts   165
When It's Time to Fire Your Agent   166
Book Contracts   167
Royalties   169
Flat Fees   170
Contractual Pitfalls   170
Royalty Statements   172
Help Is Available   173
Who Does the Index?   174
Advice from Two Publishing Law Attorneys   174

6 **Researching and Writing Your Nonfiction Book**   177

The Research You'll Need   178
Organizing Your Research   180
Writing Your Book   181
Formatting Your Manuscript   182
Organizing Your Thoughts   184
Unique Elements   186
Anecdotes, Case Studies, Quotes, and Interviews   187
Writing Style   187
Writing Mistakes   188
Submitting Your Manuscript   190
Meeting Deadlines   191
Page Proofs   191
Staying Power   192

7 **Selling Your Book to the Public**   195

The Anatomy of a Press Kit   197
What to Send to the Media and When   200
Should You Hire a Publicist?   201
When the Reviews Are Bad   202
Cautions   202
Selling the Next Book and the Book After That   203

Appendix A: Resources   204
Appendix B: References   210

Preface

I'VE SOLD, THEN written somewhere in the ballpark of fifty nonfiction books. Most have covered various career topics; some have been on how to write and get published. Without exception, I wrote a proposal for every book first, then signed a contract before I began writing. In fact, the only nonfiction book I wrote in full without a contract remains unsold. It could have been the subject matter—an English cookbook—but agents loved the idea and two tried to sell it for me over a twelve-year period. (See Chapter 4 for a look at the query letter and proposal for this cookbook.)

On the other hand, it could be that a finished nonfiction book manuscript means less involvement for the editor. When you craft a compelling book proposal that lets an editor see the possibilities, you can generate excitement that will result in a contract. Editors want to feel that you've researched their list, that you're familiar with their catalogs, and that you know exactly what they want. And if you're off target just a little bit, your proposal for your as yet unwritten book lets editors know you have an idea they can help mold.

"It's usually best not to do too much of the actual writing until the project's been accepted by a publisher," says Michael Urban, vice president at The Globe Pequot Press in Guilford, Connecticut. "Editors like to be able to shape book projects to the needs of their specific audiences."

Yes, you are expected to be aware of the specific audience of the publishers you want to approach. This way you can accurately target your proposals to the right publishers. The research you do and the proposals you write are solo acts, your responsibility. But the fine-tuning an editor will contribute to a book project makes the final result a team effort.

In the pages that follow you will learn how to find and define book ideas that will sell, how to tame those ideas into book proposals, and how to approach agents or editors with them. If all goes well—and it should—and you land a contract, this book will also help you deliver what you promise: a well-crafted, nonfiction, book-length manuscript.

Selling, then writing a nonfiction book is a commitment you make to yourself and to a process. It takes time and skill (skill that you can acquire), patience and perseverance. It is not a process for the faint of heart or the thin-skinned. You cannot be a person who gives up easily.

For those who do their homework, become familiar with the marketplace, and hone their writing skills, selling and then writing a nonfiction book is an attainable goal.

Read on.

Acknowledgments

I WOULD LIKE to thank the following professionals for their advice and insight into the world of publishing:

Nancy Abramson, Agent, Sedgeband Literary Associates, Fort Worth, Texas

Richard Balkin, Agent, The Balkin Agency, Amherst, Massachusetts

Denise Betts, Acquisitions Editor, Contemporary Books, Chicago, Illinois

Kent Carroll, Executive Editor, Carroll & Graf, New York City

David Duperre, Agent, Sedgeband Literary Associates, Fort Worth, Texas

Jessica Faust, Agent, BookEnds, Gillette, New Jersey

Ellen Geiger, Senior Agent, Curtis Brown, New York City

Roger Goldberg, Physician, Writer, Evanston, Illinois

Sara Goodman, Attorney, Parkland, Florida

Anne Hawkins, Agent, John Hawkins & Associates, New York City

Richard Henshaw, Agent, Richard Henshaw Group, New York City

Lloyd J. Jassin, Attorney, New York City

Dorian Karchmar, Agent, Lowenstein Associates, New York City

Frances Kuffel, Agent, Jean Naggar Literary Agency, New York City

Simon Lipskar, Agent, Writers House, New York City

Lori Perkins, Agent, Perkins Associates, New York City

Gail Rubin, Writer, PR Professional, Albuquerque, New Mexico

Vanda Sendzimir, Freelance Writer

Wendy Sherman, Agent, Wendy Sherman Associates, New York City

Pari Noskin Taichert, Public Relations Consultant, Albuquerque, New Mexico

Michael Urban, Vice President, The Globe Pequot Press, Guilford, Connecticut

Elizabeth Wales, Agent, Wales Literary Agency, Seattle, Washington

1

The Business of Publishing and How It Affects You

"An editor is a person who knows precisely what he wants, but isn't quite sure."

—Walter Davenport

THE FIELD OF publishing is exciting and competitive. There are risks and surprises and sometimes disappointments. Those working in this industry have a great deal of power. They determine which books and stories will see print and, to some extent, help to shape the tastes of the reading public.

In 2001, book sales totaled more than $25 billion, a 3.4 percent increase over the previous year, according to sales figures released by the Association of American Publishers (AAP). Book publishing is big business.

What type of book sells the most? Although trade sales dropped 3.7 percent overall—adult hardcover book sales experienced the largest drop, down $2.69 billion—juvenile book sales showed positive figures in both hardcover (up

13.2 percent, $1.20 billion) and paperback (up 16.4 percent, $753.1 million). Educational book sales were strong, up a significant $3.88 billion, and sales of professional and scholarly books were also positive, up $5.13 billion. Religious book sales were up slightly (2.5 percent, with sales of $1.25 billion). But university press sales mirrored the adult trade category and dropped 2.4 percent ($402 million). Mail-order publication sales showed positive numbers for the first time in two years. Book clubs were up 1.5 percent, with sales of $1.29 billion. Mass market paperback sales remained fairly even, totaling $1.56 billion.

Although an insult to art, the reality is that financial concerns often determine which books get published. When those books do well, everyone is happy—from bookstore owners to the sales team and distributors. But there are limited slots on the various bestseller lists, and, with thousands of books published each year, the odds are against producing a blockbuster. Although some books have steady sales and can stay on a publisher's backlist for years, others can disappear from bookstore shelves after only a month. All this is taken into an account when an editor or agent considers a book proposal.

Book Categories and Where Your Book Fits In

Bookstores have specific shelving systems. The surefire way to ensure your book won't get published is to pursue a title that no one will know how to shelve. Have a look in any bookstore and check out the sections. In addition to various fiction categories, you'll see (in no particular order) the following nonfiction categories:

Travel
Language
Self-help and psychology
Parenting
Relationships and sex
Science
Careers
Business
Finances
Sports
Health, fitness, and medicine
How-to

Wise Words

Writing is the incurable itch that possesses many.

—Juvenal

Humor
Art and architecture
Food and cooking
History
Hobby and craft
Home and garden
Computers
Music
History and military
Politics and government
Agriculture
Astrology and New Age
Autobiographies and memoirs
Biographies
Fashion and beauty
Reference
Regional
Spiritual
Technical
True crime
Women's issues

Some bookstores will have even more categories; others will have fewer. The important point, though, is for you to see where your idea would be shelved. Could you state with certainty what genre your book is? You'll need to be able to do that when you meet with agents or editors at writers' conferences and when you propose your idea in your query letter and book proposal. See Chapter 3 for more information on presenting your book idea professionally.

What's Hot, What's Not

One bestseller list at the time of this writing features the following ten titles:

> *The Prayer of Jabez* by Bruce Wilkinson (Multnomah)
> *Who Moved My Cheese?* by Spencer Johnson (Penguin USA)
> *John Adams* by David McCullough (Simon & Schuster)
> *The Wild Blue* by Stephen E. Ambrose (Simon & Schuster)
> *Crossing Over* by John Edward (Jodere Group)
> *Body for Life* by Bill Phillips (HarperCollins)
> *The Road to Wealth: A Comprehensive Guide to Your Money—*
>   *Everything You Need to Know in Good and Bad Times* by
>   Suze Orman (Riverhead Books)
> *Call Me Crazy* by Anne Heche (Scribner)
> *Fish! A Remarkable Way to Boost Morale and Improve Results*
>   by Stephen Lundin (Hyperion)
> *Living a Life That Matters* by Harold S. Kushner
>   (A. A. Knopf)

Four fall into the inspirational/self-help category; two are celebrity memoirs; two are historical biographies; one covers financial matters; and another talks about health and fitness. A look at any bestseller list for a given week will consistently reflect the nation's interest in these same topics.

What Publishers Are Looking For

"I think every editor in town is looking for the next *Longitude* or *The Professor and the Madman*," says agent Anne Hawkins (John Hawkins & Associates). "Well-told stories of extraordinary people or events are always hot."

Wise Words

The shelf life of the modern hardback writer is somewhere between the milk and the yogurt.

—John Mortimer

Wise Words

Any writer, I suppose, feels that the world into which he was born is nothing less than a conspiracy against the cultivation of his talent.

—James Baldwin

"Hottest right now is narrative nonfiction," states senior agent Ellen Geiger (Curtis Brown). "That is, true-life stories that read like a novel, as with *The Perfect Storm* or *A Civil Action*. An author with a fresh subject and excellent credentials will sell. Good journalists who want to expand on a great story they may have covered for a magazine or newspaper are likely to sell. Overdone subjects such as alternative health, fitness, and relationship books may be harder to place."

David Duperre, an agent with Sedgeband Literary Associates, adds, "At present, self-help, health, and true crime are our hottest nonfiction material."

Agent Jessica Faust (BookEnds) says, "Every editor is looking for the next revolutionary author, the next Suze Orman or Dean Ornish."

Dorian Karchmar, an agent with Lowenstein Associates, explains, "I wouldn't say that anything is an inherently 'easy' sell—in other words, even if a particular subject is hot, it's still all in the execution. That said, I think there is still a strong interest in narrative nonfiction, nonfiction that both teaches readers something (about a particular historical event, a scientific discovery, an arcane or exotic profession) and keeps them entertained.

"*Longitude: The True Story of a Lone Genius Who Solved the Greatest Scientific Problem of His Time* by Dava Sobel really opened up this world of narrative nonfiction, which continues to flourish with titles as diverse as Simon Winchester's *The Professor and the Madman*, Peter Mayle's *A Year in Provence*, and the list goes on."

"Adventure narrative is selling well now," says Globe Pequot Press vice president Michael Urban. He should know—his house publishes mainly travel and outdoor recreation titles.

Dorian Karchmar agrees. "Adventure narrative is hot," she says, "though I think the mountain adventures spawned by Krakauer, and the seafaring

"In some companies editors have been told not to sign up anything that can't be counted on to hit at least 50,000 or some other arbitrary figure. Another command from on high is 'buy only bestsellers.'"

—Paul Nathan, *The Golden Age of Opportunity*

adventures (Sebastian Junger and the many books about Shackleton and other doomed historical expeditions) have, perhaps, run their course. Now it's fire, volcanoes—natural disaster."

Who's Publishing Nonfiction

Between 75 and 85 percent of all books published in the United States and Canada today are produced by about eight megacorporations and a dozen or so of the largest independent publishers. After the big guys, another 2,200 publishers or so are listed by the U.S. Commerce Bureau. *Literary Market Place*, published by R. R. Bowker, names another 18,000 to 20,000 smaller and independent publishers. This section shows how book publishers are categorized and the type of attention you'll get within each category.

National/International Publishers

These are the eight megaconglomerates that rule book publishing in the Western Hemisphere, followed by some of their major imprints in parentheses. Many of these publishers must be approached through a literary agent (more on that in Chapter 3).

1. Hearst Corporation (Avon, William Morrow)
2. News Corporation/Rupert Murdock (HarperCollins)
3. Pearson PLC (Penguin USA, G. P. Putnam, Berkley)
4. Viacom (Simon & Schuster, Pocket Books)
5. Advance/Newhouse (Random House, A. A. Knopf, Modern Library, Ballentine)

6. Bertelsmann AG (Bantam, Doubleday, Dell, Dial)
7. Time Warner/Ted Turner (Little Brown, Book of the Month)
8. Holtzbrinck (Farrar, Straus & Giroux, St. Martin's Press, Henry Holt)

If you're lucky enough to get your book proposal accepted by one of these giants, you may find that your advance is handsomer than what some of the smaller presses could offer. They may issue a bigger print run for your book, too, suggesting that sales figures could go higher than with a small press.

You'd think with one of these megacorporations that you'd get a sizable budget for promotion—but that isn't necessarily so. Big budgets go to the books that salespeople and top editors decide in advance to single out for stardom. If your book isn't on the star track, you shouldn't expect a whirlwind book tour with appearances on Leno.

Once your book is out, you might find you're fading to the back of the room. Editors at big houses have a lot of projects to work on and a lot of authors in their stables. You probably won't get the individual attention you'd like. But it certainly is heady having the logo of a big publishing house on the jacket of your first book.

Regional/Small Presses

"The literary giants of tomorrow are probably being published by small presses today," said Karin Taylor, executive director of The Small Press Center, quoted in *The Writer* several years ago. And she's probably right. Literary giants don't necessarily reveal themselves right away—and the big publishers are reluctant to take chances on unknown writers.

There are thousands of independent book publishers, most of whom never see themselves mentioned in the *New York Times Book Review* or on the bestseller list. But these small presses can take chances; they don't need megahits to survive. They know how to reach specialty and special interest markets and specific regions of the country. They choose to publish the books that will appeal to those markets.

Small press and regional publishers release fewer titles a year, their print runs are smaller, and so are sales. Staff might consist of one or two people wearing many hats, from editor and publisher to errand runner and mail clerk.

You can often approach these presses without a literary agent, and, once in, you'll find yourself getting more individual attention.

University Presses

Generally, university presses specialize in particular subjects, often educational in nature, but many also publish mainstream books. Most enjoy fine reputations and give each project professional care and individual attention. In addition, most can be approached without an agent. But promotion budgets are generally small or nonexistent.

Organizational/Sponsored Presses

Many associations and other organizations have their own publishing section, producing books that are of interest to their members, clients, or field. A professional association dealing with adoption, for example, might produce a nonfiction how-to or a novel with an adoption theme. The first publisher for Tom Clancy's *The Hunt for Red October* was the Naval Institute Press.

You can approach these presses without an agent, but don't expect impressive advances or print runs. Publicity outside the targeted organization would most likely be your own responsibility.

Subsidy Publishers

While traditional publishers are always overrun with manuscript submissions, subsidy publishers have to advertise their need for manuscripts. It's the writers who pay the subsidy publishers, not the reading public.

Subsidy publishers are also known as vanity presses because they prey on writers who have not been able to break in yet—and on writers who just don't know any better. They present themselves as commercial publishers, offering to evaluate your manuscript (all manuscripts are accepted) and offering a publishing contract. But when it comes time for payment, you pay the publisher instead of advances and royalties coming to you.

Subsidy publishers do put a manuscript into print. Some offer minimal help with marketing. But libraries and book reviewers recognize subsidy publishing when they see it and won't buy or review those books.

It's best to avoid this route. If you have a book worth publishing, a real publisher will pay you for it, not the other way around.

Cooperative Publishers

Some publishers ask authors to share the cost of producing the book. The author might pay for part of the cost of printing and binding, for example, or provide the typeset, camera-ready copy. Writers who participate in cooperative publishing are sharing the risk that is usually the publisher's alone.

Some small publishers work in three categories, publishing some books on a commercial basis, some through a co-op arrangement, and others through author subsidy. The stigma of vanity publishing still attaches itself to some cooperative publishers—especially those who also work on a subsidy basis. The same warning for writers applies here as to subsidy publishers.

Book Packagers/Producers

This fairly new breed of publishing is on the rise. Book packagers, or book producers as they are sometimes called, act as go-betweens, selling a concept to a publisher and then contracting with a writer to create the book. More often than not, the author works for a set (work-for-hire) fee rather than receiving royalties. The book packager generally holds the copyright to the book. These aren't terms in the writer's favor.

In an article previously published on the Authorlink website, current agent and former book packager Jessica Faust says:

> A book packager is a cross between an agent and an editor, and more. A book packager often works with agents, authors, editors, designers, illustrators, photographers, and printers—all of the people who make a book possible. By working with such a variety of people, a book packager has the ability to deliver a printer-ready manuscript to the publisher. That means that once the publisher receives the final product it has already been written and edited, pictures have been supplied, production people have been called in to lay out the book, and the entire project is ready to be sent to the printer.
>
> Much like an agent, a book packager submits manuscripts to an editor at a publishing house. These manuscripts are usually prepared in either of two ways:
>
> 1. The project has been requested by the publisher. The book packager puts together an outline and finds a writer interested in authoring the book.
>
> 2. The concept is developed "in-house" (within the book packaging company). An outline and sample materials are put together—with or without an author—and the material is sent to the publisher.

Then, just as if a writer or his or her agent were to submit a proposal to a publisher, the packager waits for that fateful phone call and checks the mailbox for rejections.

Once an editor agrees to buy or publish a project, the process starts from the top. The packager works with the author to develop a well-written book and turns in the edited manuscript to the publisher.

Self-Publishing

Self-publishers are responsible for every aspect of the publication of their own material: writing and editing it, designing page layout, choosing the cover copy and colors, getting the printing done, arranging for distribution, and handling publicity and sales. It can be very risky business, and it can carry the same sort of stigma that attaches itself to vanity and cooperative publishing. There is a handful of self-publishing success stories, but compared with the billions of dollars of books published each year, that handful is pretty small.

Writers with nonfiction projects and easy-to-reach audiences have the best chance with self-publishing. In other words, if you're a nutritionist and you frequently give seminars and talks and can sell your book as part of the seminar tuition, then go for it. If your book is aimed at a larger audience—all women, for example, or all children—self-publishing would not be the way to go. Wide audiences are hard to reach. Narrow topics and narrow audiences offer the best scenario for self-publishers.

Electronic Publishing

Electronic publishing is emerging as an alternative delivery system for books—or so they say. The options mentioned here do exist, but nobody knows whether anyone is making any money at it.

In theory, people pay for, then download material. They either read the material on their computer screen or a handheld device designed for this purpose, or they print out individual copies of the work. This print on demand is carried out at some bookstores or in the customers' homes.

Some electronic publishers act as the online equivalent to subsidy and cooperative publishers, charging writers for webspace and uploading and not providing any real marketing help. Many of them do not edit the material and accept every manuscript that comes their way. Other online publishers are trying to be selective and publish only books they feel are worthy.

Many traditional publishing houses have created websites to promote their traditionally published books. One such publisher tried an experiment, providing a Stephen King serial only to online customers. Another followed suit—but then the fad rolled to a halt. The question is, Will these cyberbooks ever become more than a fad? Again, no real figures are available to back up the claims electronic publishers make.

For writers, the online option might seem an easy avenue to publication and less expensive than working with a vanity press. And there are no more stacks of books sitting in the garage. But again, there's that stigma.

The National Writers Union (NWU) offers guidelines to help writers navigate their way through this rapidly changing industry. The guidelines assert that the right to publish the electronic version of any book should be negotiated. These rights should be retained by the creator of the work unless they are specifically stated in the contract. Some publishers claim that electronic versions of a book are simply extensions of the print rights. The NWU's position, recently reinforced by the Supreme Court decision in *Tasini v. the New York Times*, is that electronic versions of any book are not extensions of print rights; an E-book is a different version altogether (the same as movie rights, audio rights, and so on) and should be a separate item negotiated in the contract.

Frontlists, Midlists, and Backlists

While doing your research, reading market guides and publishers' guidelines, you'll most likely run across a few terms that are new to you. *Frontlist, midlist,* and *backlist* come up frequently. Contemporary Books editor Denise Betts provides definitions that clear up the mystery:

> First of all, writers should not get too hung up on these labels. Sometimes writers get offended because they think if their book is a midlist book, it means it's not as important to the publisher as they feel it should be. Not every book can receive top billing as a frontlist book, and it's the sum of all the published titles that contributes to the prestige of a publishing program.
>
> Frontlist titles are featured with larger spreads in the catalog, may receive more marketing and publicity efforts, and generally have high-profile authors attached to them.

Midlist titles are those that will be modest, but probably steady, sellers during the life of the book. These books generally receive fewer marketing efforts, and publicity will probably consist of a targeted mailing to relevant print and media channels.

Backlist titles are a publisher's bread and butter. These are titles that may not sell tens of thousands of copies in the first year but might do so over the course of several years. Typically, these books are not so timely in nature that they will date quickly, and they do not capitalize on a fad. They are on evergreen topics always of interest to the book-buying public.

The main characteristics of the backlist book are that it stays in print for a long time and generally turns a decent profit for the publisher and the author. Backlist books are considered a safe bet for a publisher, and writers may want to focus their energies on creating ideas that will fall into this category.

Who to Approach

There are many publishing options open to the nonfiction writer. For the most part, the type of book you are proposing will dictate what type of publisher you'll end up approaching. A university press might not be interested in a fancy coffee-table book, for example, while one of the megapublishers would probably pass on an anthropological study of a small tribe in West Africa.

To identify the right publishers for your project, find the names of publishing houses that put out work similar to yours. Look through bookstores, library shelves, and market guides such as *Writer's Market* and *Literary Market Place*. You'll find more information on these books in Appendix B.

The Internet can also help in your search. These days most major publishers and many small presses have websites where you can order books, examine their catalogs, and get an idea of the type of books they publish. Some provide guidelines for writers on their websites, saving you the trouble of sending a written request. To find the publishers you're interested in, call up any search engine (such as Yahoo or Excite), and type in key words such as *book publishers* or the specific house you'd like to visit. Some may have obvious web addresses—www.mcgrawhill.com, for example. Others you'll have to search for.

There's more, though. Once you've created your wish list of publishing houses, you'll need to identify the editors within each house. Who handles what? Editors and the subject areas with which they work are listed in the previously mentioned market guides. The publisher's guidelines will also help

> Always request a publisher's guidelines before querying that publisher. Guidelines provide a wealth of information, including topics accepted, word count, and more. Type up a simple request ("May I please have a copy of your guidelines for writers?") and send it out with a #10 business-size, self-addressed, stamped envelope (SASE).

narrow the field; the names of the acquisitions editors for particular subject areas are usually listed.

Knowing your topic and how to categorize it, being familiar with the type of publishers who routinely work in that area, and identifying editors who acquire in your field will help nail your chances of selling your book.

Working with an Agent

Both beginning and advanced writers share a multitude of concerns when it comes to finding and working with an agent. The following most frequently asked questions address those concerns.

1. Do I really need an agent?

For fiction, it's a good idea. These days most of the big publishing houses refuse to consider unsolicited manuscripts. If you send in your manuscript on your own, it will most likely be returned unread (if you remembered to enclose an SASE). A polite form letter might accompany it, suggesting you find an agent.

Many publishers credit agents with the ability to screen out inappropriate submissions. An agent is expected to be familiar with the different kinds of books publishers prefer to take on. New writers don't always take the time to research this information. A knowledgeable agent won't send a romance novel to a publisher who handles only science fiction, whereas a new writer might.

Having an agent also gives you a psychological edge with publishers. If an agent liked your project enough to take you on as a client, there must be some merit to it.

For nonfiction, especially with most of the smaller houses, having an agent isn't as important. Writers can send their query letters and proposals to the appropriate editors at these houses; most are used to working with unagented writers.

But if your nonfiction topic seems a great match for the big guys, an agent should be who you approach first.

2. What do agents do?

Having an agent frees you, the writer, to do what you do best—write. The agent's job is to find the right house for your work and, once successful, to negotiate the best deal for you. He or she is familiar with contracts and knows the pitfalls to avoid.

Agents are trained to recognize good or bad writing and can also spot a diamond in the rough. Some agents will work with their clients to get almost-ready manuscripts to a saleable level. Others expect manuscripts to be in market-ready condition before the writers approach them. In any event, an agent will not submit a manuscript that isn't ready to publishers, whereas new writers often rush to send out their work before taking the time to polish and edit.

Agents must also keep good financial records and maintain separate bank accounts for each client. They generally receive advances and royalty checks from the publishers for their clients and must disburse those funds as they come in.

An agent can also provide you with encouragement and validation. In the seemingly never-ending struggle for publication, isn't it nice to have someone in your corner?

3. But isn't finding an agent as difficult as finding a publisher?

Agents are always on the lookout for new talent. That's how they earn their living. If you are getting only rejection slips from agents you are approaching, there are three possible reasons:

1. The agent is too overcommitted to take on any new writers. (This might be a temporary situation. Down the road, the agent might be more receptive.)

2. You have approached the wrong agent for your genre. It pays to do a little homework first. Writer's Digest Books publishes the *Guide to Literary Agents*. A category index lists the different subject areas, and cross-referenced under each agent's listing is his or her interest area. It's a waste of everyone's time and your postage if you submit a science fiction manuscript to an agent who handles only romance or mainstream.

3. If you have targeted the right agents but are still getting rejections, it might be time to revise that query letter (help for that is in Chapter 3) or refine your book idea. Or go on to the next project. That last bit of advice might be hard to swallow, but your query letter is meant as a miniproposal whose function is to pinpoint interest in your topic before you write the book. It's better to find out early on if the interest isn't there.

4. I've found an agent, but how do I know it's the right one for me?

Ideally, your prospective agent—and any agent you approach with the hope of representation—should be a member of the Association of Authors' Representatives (AAR). Membership reassures you that the agent has agreed to adhere to the AAR canon of ethics, which has several important points. One, in particular, restricts the charging of fees:

> . . . the practice of literary agents charging clients or potential clients for reading and evaluating literary works (including outlines, proposals, and partial or complete manuscripts) is subject to serious abuse that reflects adversely on our profession. For that reason, members may not charge clients or potential clients for reading and evaluating literary works and may not benefit, directly or indirectly, from the charging for such services by any other person or entity. The term "charge" in the previous sentence includes any request for payment other than to cover the actual cost of returning materials.

In other words, the job of an agent is to sell the work of a writer to a publisher. If the agent makes his or her income from editing or evaluating work, then a conflict of interest enters into the equation. Why should an agent who's successful at earning evaluation fees bother to expend the energy looking for a publisher for the work?

Having said that, editing or suggesting changes is often an important part of an agent's job. This is something that agents do when they decide to take on a project that still needs some work. They work directly with the writer, making notes, suggesting changes and improvements. This is not a conflict of interest; it's a conflict only if the agent charges for the service.

Some unscrupulous "agents" (anyone can hang out a shingle and call himself or herself an agent) have even made false promises to writers: "Pay for my editing service and I'll agree to take you on as a client. I'll get you published if you pay for the editing." Some have joined forces with some not-so-scrupulous book doctors/editors and refer writers to these editors—then receive a commission for each referral.

For every rule, there is an exception—and there is an exception to the policy of charging fees. The following statement is also found in the AAR canon of ethics:

> In addition to the compensation for agency services that is agreed upon between a member and a client, a member may, subject to the approval of the client, pass along charges incurred by the member on the client's behalf, such as copyright fees, manuscript retyping, photocopies, copies of books for use in the sale of other rights, long distance calls, special messenger fees, etc. Such charges shall be made only if the client has agreed to reimburse such expenses.

Some agents pass these charges on to a client only after they've made a sale for that client—no sale, no charges. Others charge for photocopying right up front; still others may have clients make their own manuscript copies. It boils down to what overhead expenses an agency believes it's responsible for and what should be charged individually to the client.

AAR member agents must act ethically in all professional matters and avoid any conflicts of interest. Not every nonmember agent is unscrupulous, though. Agents must be in practice for eighteen months before the AAR will bestow membership. They must also sell a certain amount of work before they can join. Says the AAR:

> Associate members of AAR are full-time employees of an agency member. They do not yet qualify for full membership but are actively engaged in the selling of rights and are working toward qualifying.

Full membership requirements are available in the AAR bylaws. If you're interested, contact the Association of Authors' Representatives at P.O. Box

237201, Ansonia Station, New York, NY 10003, or visit their website at pub-lishersweekly.com/aar. You'll find the full AAR canon of ethics at the web-site plus a membership list.

5. *Shouldn't an agent send me an agent-author contract as soon as he or she has agreed to take me on?*

Some will; some will discuss their terms with you verbally or in a letter of intent, then attach an addendum to the publisher's contract for any sales they might make on your behalf. The addendum will specify the commission, normally 15 percent for domestic sales and 20 percent for foreign. This is a perfectly legiti-mate and common way of operating. However, more and more agents have standard contracts they use, and more and more writers insist on it.

Turn to Chapter 5 for more information on contracts.

6. *Will an agent make allowances for my inexperience?*

In some areas, yes; in some areas, no. Providing inappropriate information in a query letter ("All my friends love my manuscript," "You should be able to get me a lot of money for this one," and so on), for example, might not impress an agent the way you had hoped, but if your work stands out, such gaffes in the query letter will be overlooked. (For some agents, that is. Oth-ers will be so put off, they won't read further.)

Expecting an agent to provide extensive editing to your manuscript is unrealistic. Occasionally an agent spots a real diamond in the rough and is willing to go the extra mile, but most just don't have the time. You should sub-mit the best work you can—then look forward to a long, productive rela-tionship with your new agent.

How Literary Agencies Are Structured

Some literary agents choose to work on their own, with little more than sec-retarial assistance. They can rent space in an office building or work from a home office. Other agents prefer to work within an established agency, as either the owner or one of the associates. This way, they can still function independently, choosing the writers and book projects they want to work with. In an agency, agents usually must contribute a percentage of their income to cover the office's operating expenses.

Location, Location, Location

At one time, agents worked only in New York City, which is where most of the major publishing houses are. But this is changing rapidly. Agents are now located all over the country. Telephones, faxes, E-mail, and numerous commuter flights make business possible no matter where the agent hangs his or her shingle.

However, there still is some stigma attached to non–New York locations. It's important, though, not to confuse a small, isolated location with a poor agent. If an agent is up on current publishing trends, knows his or her business, and is well read and well informed, location isn't as important. But if the agent's practices reflect something less than professionalism—submitting substandard manuscripts or submitting manuscripts to the wrong houses, for example—the location as well as the agent may be blamed.

In truth, there are good agents and not-so-good agents. And some of those not-so-good agents work and live right in New York City.

How to Find an Agent

Most literary agents generally do not advertise for clients. (Be wary of those who do.) They provide information for listings in a variety of guides—the *Guide to Literary Agents*, *Literary Market Place*, and *Writer's Guide to Book Editors, Publishers, and Literary Agents* by Jeff Herman (see Appendix B). Agents also frequently attend writers' conferences and meet with prospective clients there (see Chapter 3).

Some agents have websites where they can post writers' guidelines and their wish lists—the type of material they'd like to represent. Be careful about submitting work to agents you find on the Internet. Some very legitimate and respectable agents have websites. But some unscrupulous ones do, too. Make sure you approach only AAR member agents.

Agent Dorian Karchmar sums it up well: "Get an agent with a track record, yes, but an agent who is still energetic and who loves your work. Enthusiasm is contagious."

Twelve Questions to Ask When Choosing an Agent

An agent is only as good as his or her word. An agent's reputation—both good and bad—can spread quickly through the writing community. With more and more writers' associations and Internet connections, writers are not as isolated as they once were. They talk to each other and exchange information. New writers learn what to look for in an agent.

Although it would be inappropriate to interview an agent before he or she has seen your work and asked to represent you, once the offer is made, it is your turn to make sure the agent is the best one for you. Here's a list of questions you can ask a prospective agent:

1. Do you have agents at your agency or subagents working in Hollywood or overseas who handle movie and television rights? Foreign rights?

2. Will you be solely responsible for my work, or will another associate in your firm handle my work?

3. Do you have an agent-author agreement or contract? (See Chapter 5 for more information on contracts.)

4. How do you keep clients up-to-date on your activities on their behalf? Will you let me know who you are sending my work to and what their responses are? Do you call with rejections; do you mail copies of all correspondence? Is it OK if I call you occasionally?

5. Do you confer with your clients on all offers that are made?

6. What percentage commission do you charge? What are your policies about charging for normal overhead expenses such as photocopying and messengers?

7. Are you a member of AAR?

8. What's your track record? Have you sold books to established publishers? Were any in my genre?

9. Will you make simultaneous submissions for me, or send to only one publisher at a time?

10. Are you familiar and skilled with the auction process?

11. How many clients do you currently represent? (Fifty is about average. Any more and you start getting lost in the crowd.)

12. What is your policy for ending the agent-author relationship? Is this stated in your agent-author contract? (See Chapter 5 for tips on how to end the agent-author relationship.)

2

Finding and Defining Book Ideas That Sell

"There are only two or three human stories, and they go on repeating themselves as fiercely as if they had never happened before."

—Willa Cather

WHAT WRITER, NEW or seasoned, doesn't dream of coming up with the next bestselling book idea? Oh, to be Simon Winchester, author of *The Professor and the Madman*, or David McCullough, author of *John Adams* and *Truman*. Both made it to the bestseller list, as have many others.

But the bestseller list isn't always the goal for a new writer, nor should it be. While there are only ten to fifteen slots on the various lists at any one time, there are thousands of nonfiction books published every year. Close to 60,000 books will come out this year, and 85 to 90 percent of those books will be nonfiction. That's around 51,000 to 54,000 opportunities for one of those books to be yours. Not bad odds, and much better than those for fiction writers. Only 10 to 15 percent of books published each year are novels, and it's much harder for a new writer to break into the fiction arena.

Finding Book Ideas

Book ideas are everywhere. You can find them in newspaper headlines or in the back pages, covering more obscure events or human interest stories.

Study bookstore shelves and see what's showing up there. Which books are housed cover out? Which show only the spine? Then look for the gaps—what's missing?

Analyze bestseller lists, as discussed in Chapter 1. What trends do you see?

Talk with librarians. They have a wonderful sense of what the reading public wants. What do readers routinely ask for?

Look into specialty book clubs—not Book-of-the-Month-Club types that handle mainly fiction, but clubs that cater to a specific audience or a specific nonfiction reading taste such as military history or science.

Ask publishers directly; they'll tell you what they need. They may not have time to talk to you person to person, and an investigative phone call would probably not be the best idea early on. But if you send away for their catalogs and guidelines, you'll see what they publish and where the holes in their lists might be. Catalogs are usually free, although publishers prefer to receive a #10 business-size, self-addressed, stamped envelope (SASE) for guideline requests. These days, many publishers also maintain websites and post their guidelines there. Do a thorough online search.

When the catalogs arrive, devour them. You'll see you don't have to come up with your own original idea. By looking through publishers' catalogs, you can see those who publish series. Could you write a Dummies book or an Idiot's Guide? Explore how you might contribute to an existing line of books.

Ten Steps to Judge the Merit of Your Ideas

As you can imagine, there are countless book ideas to explore (although author Willa Cather said, "There are only two or three human stories, and they go on repeating themselves as fiercely as if they had never happened before"). But how do you know whether what you've come up with is a *good* book idea, whether it's saleable? H. L. Mencken said, "There are no dull subjects. There are only dull writers."

Look at your book idea using these steps and you'll have a better handle on whether it deserves more work.

1. Decide whether your idea is meaty enough to deserve a full-length manuscript and the full-sized price tag that will come along with it. Could a magazine-length article possibly do the subject justice? Are you sure there are a lot of people willing to plunk down $15 to $30 for your book?

Test your idea by submitting related articles to magazines covering your topic. If the response is favorable, you might even get an article or two slated for publication.

2. Talk to bookstore personnel and librarians. They have their fingers on the reading pulse of America and can give you a thumbs-up on your topic if it would be of interest to their patrons.

3. Identify the competition by doing a thorough search for similar books in *Books in Print*. This publication is now online at booksinprint.com. It is the most complete and accurate source for more than 4 million book-related records, including 1.6 million active book titles, 1.9 million out-of-print titles, 250,000 video titles, and 150,000 audio book titles.

Also check online at Amazon.com or *Publishers Weekly*, which lists all the upcoming books. See whether your book covers an angle that competing titles neglect.

4. Focus your idea tightly to cover this important angle. For example, a book on parenting from birth through age eighteen would be too wide, whereas something on the teen years might just hit home.

Wise Words

Great writers arrive among us like new diseases—threatening, powerful, impatient for patients to pick up their virus, irresistible.

—Craig Raine

Avoid too narrow a focus as well. The first week in the life of an infant might be interesting but covers too little ground to appeal to many readers. The first six months or, even better, the first year might make an easier sale.

5. In performing the research suggested in item 3, you may find there is no competition in print. This could be good—you're poised to be first in line. Or there could be a reason there are no competing titles; for example, your search was faulty or there is no interest in your topic in the marketplace. The only way to know is to go back to item 2 and test your idea again.

6. Ask yourself whether your idea is fresh and original. Instead of a new slant on an old topic, have you come up with something revolutionary, something bound to hook reader interest and find a place on a bookstore shelf?

7. Make sure your idea is promotable. Know who your intended audience is and how to reach it. Agent Jessica Faust (BookEnds) says she'd love to represent "someone with a platform and new ideas. Someone who already comes with a built-in audience."

8. Determine whether you have the qualifications to write your book. You don't necessarily have to be an expert, but you should feel you're the best person for this particular job. In addition, you need good research skills and—obviously—the ability to write.

9. Your idea should be something you feel strongly about. Kent Carroll, executive editor at Carroll & Graf, says, "You should have the need to write. And you should write about things that are important to you, what you believe in, what you have passion about." If your idea becomes a published book, it's a topic you'll potentially be living and breathing for a long time.

If you are excited about your subject matter, you might be able to spread that passion to others. Agent Wendy Sherman, of Wendy Sherman Associates, says, "I'm being very careful what I take on. I only want to represent what I feel completely passionate about."

Says agent Simon Lipskar (Writers House), "Books such as *The Professor and the Madman* are what I love."

Wise Words

The secret of good writing is to say an old thing in a new way or to say a new thing in an old way.

—Richard Harding Davis

---

10. Ask yourself whether you possess the qualities necessary to be successful in this field. Are you a persistent and patient person, in this for the long haul? Are you realistic? Do you understand that even if your idea is accepted and your book gets published, chances are you won't become rich or famous? Knowing this, do you still want to go ahead with it?

Go through these steps carefully and keep good notes as you do your research. You will find that the process of refining and evaluating your idea will provide excellent material for the query letter and book proposal you'll soon have to write (see Chapter 3).

Advice from Publishing Professionals on Selling Your Nonfiction Book

Agent Anne Hawkins

"Choose your topic very carefully. Make sure it's one where you have the interest and expertise to write a credible proposal. Research comparable books. If it looks like the market is saturated with publications on similar topics, go back to the drawing board. Nonfiction sells because the concept is fresh and the author is the ideal person to write about it!"

Agent Jessica Faust

"Know the market! You need to know what your competition is and how your book differs. If your book isn't that different and there are already thirty books out there on the same subject, then it isn't going to be easy to sell the book. If necessary, make up a page describing the marketing potential of your book and how it is different from the perceived competition."

Senior Agent Ellen Geiger

"Have a realistic grasp of your background, skills, and experience. Try to develop a marketing and distribution strategy before you approach agents. One of the first questions editors ask about a potential project is, What is the author's platform? That is, how is he or she going to get the word out about the book? What is his or her network? What strategies—websites, speaking engagements, workshops, classes, and so on—can be used? Everyone can't be a guest on Oprah, at least not right away."

Agent David Duperre

"Find out first if anyone would be interested in the type of book you want to write. If something similar hasn't been published, then there is probably a reason. Query editors and agents, tell them your idea, and see what they think. If they tell you they like it and think it will sell, then get to work. But if they tell you they're not interested or that it's just not what they want, then it may not be a good idea to spend your time writing the manuscript."

Vice President Michael Urban

"Be patient, be persistent, and be open to suggestions on how to improve your proposed book."

Identifying Trends and Avoiding Fads

"Book publishing is such a fluid market that what is hot today might not be hot tomorrow," says agent Jessica Faust. Learning to tell the difference between a fad and a trend could mean the difference between getting published or not. It can often take a year or more from the time your proposal is accepted to when your book will see print. A topic that's timely when you start out could very easily fade from interest by the time your story would hit

---

Wise Words

To write what is worth publishing, to find honest people
to publish it, and to get sensible people to read it are the
three great difficulties in being an author.

—Charles Caleb Colton

---

the bookstores. Publishers know this, but new writers often do not take this
into account.

A fad is a flash in the pan, and although someone probably did get his
or her idea into print, the chances of copycat or "me too" books having the
same luck are not very high. O. J. Simpson books fall into the exception-to-
the-rule category. What should have been a passing fad turned into a multi-
million-dollar business in 1995, with fifty books released in that year alone.
More have followed and will follow in the years ahead.

A trend has more staying power than a fad. It could last for a decade or
longer and cover areas such as health, fitness, relationships, and more. Avoiding the fads and getting in on a trend—or even starting one—is the ideal place
to be. Dr. Atkins, for example, hit the lists with a high-fat, low-carbohydrate
diet book and started a new trend. Dieters were tired of all the no-fat diets, so
he offered what people wanted when they wanted it. Now using hormones and
metabolics, addressing body types, and "mastering the zone" to burn fat have
become popular weight-loss trends.

However, just as no one can predict a bestseller, no one can predict a new
trend. There's a lot to be said for luck and being in the right place at the right
time. But a little educated guessing and a lot of market savvy can put you in
that place. Following are some tips for determining whether your idea is a
one-night stand or has long-term staying power:

- The idea keeps burning in you for a long time. You put it aside for a
  while, but it still looks good when you come back to it.

- Your idea has a hook that will grab readers' attention—and remember, your first readers are agents or editors. It's got a twist or new angle on an old idea that is original and fresh, something to get excited about.
- Your idea isn't too timely. Interest is unlikely to fade by the time your book sees print.
- Your idea will fill a gap in the marketplace. There's a real need for your book; it's not just a piece of fluff.

If you're still worried about identifying a trend—don't be. Two agents give some good advice on the subject:

- Elizabeth Wales (Wales Literary Agency): "Don't chase trends. Write about what you care about and are drawn to."
- Richard Henshaw (Richard Henshaw Group): "Don't try to guess the trends. . . . Write what you feel passionately about, but if you want to sell, keep an eye on what is commercially viable in your niche."

Who Can Sell, Then Write a Nonfiction Book?

"Writing is not the lottery," says agent Lori Perkins of Perkins Associates. "New writers have to be realistic about what it takes to get published. But there is one similarity to the lottery: you have to play to win."

So, you've been playing. You've found and defined your book idea, and narrowed and slanted your focus. You've tested that idea and determined it will stand up over time. You've done your research and identified any competition. You know your proposed book will fill a gap in the marketplace.

You've combed bookstore shelves and market guidebooks and sent away for publishers' catalogs and guidelines. You know exactly to whom you'll be submitting your idea, and you're getting ready to write your query letter and proposal. In fact, the only section left to tackle is listing your qualifications for writing this book. Should be a piece of cake, right? Maybe not. Not only do you have to sell your idea, but also you have to sell yourself and convince publishers you are the best person to write about this idea.

Does a writer have to be an expert in the field to sell a nonfiction book? "There's just no yes-or-no answer to this question," says agent Anne Hawkins. "It depends on the nature of the project. For example, with certain kinds of seri-

---

Wise Words

How vain it is to sit down to write when you have not stood up to live.

—Henry David Thoreau

---

ous nonfiction, especially books that target both the trade and academic markets, an author's expert credentials are absolutely essential. Also, books giving prescriptive advice on health issues are best left to professionals in the field."

Agent Dorian Karchmar agrees. "Self-help, parenting, psychology, relationships, diet, and exercise—you must be an expert. Areas in which there's a real glut in the market, not only do you need to be an expert, you need to have a means of helping promote the book: a 'platform' (a mailing list, your own organization, media contacts, lectures, workshops, seminars, and so on). Otherwise there's simply not going to be any way of getting attention for it, of making it stand out from the rest."

Senior agent Ellen Geiger states, "Where New York trade publishing is concerned, the answer is pretty much yes. You must be an expert—*expert* as in having very good credentials, not necessarily having to be Madame Curie. Having lived through the topic—as in battling diseases or overcoming loss— is rarely enough, unless the writing is excellent and the story overwhelmingly compelling and fresh."

Contemporary Books editor Denise Betts says, "In some cases, yes; in others, no. If the writer is tackling a subject such as the latest branding trend, then he or she should probably be a high-profile marketing industry expert. If the project is a small gift book on ways to show your child you love her, then you might not need to be the next Dr. Spock, just a good writer with a good idea. It all depends on the subject matter and the needs and requirements of the publishing house."

Experts on the Bestseller Lists

Let's look again at the bestseller list on page 4. The top ten books on the list showcase authors who fall into the following categories:

- Two religious leaders (writing on inspirational topics)
- Two historians (writing on historical topics)
- Two motivational writers (writing parables as prescriptions for a better life)
- Two celebrities (writing memoirs)
- One bodybuilding magazine publisher (writing on bodybuilding)
- One financial expert (writing on money matters)

All are either multipublished experts in their various fields or well-known celebrities—not one newcomer in the bunch. That doesn't mean a new author couldn't land on the nonfiction bestseller list, but it tells us it's more likely that a writer can find a bestseller slot after accumulating more experience.

That aside, the bestseller list is not every writer's dream. At least, not at first. Most new writers would be happy just to get that first book out there. Can a nonexpert land a contract? Yes, of course. Read on.

Making Yourself More Saleable

One way to give yourself credibility for your book project is to get an expert to work with you. Find someone well known in the field and request that this person write a foreword or an introduction for you. Better yet, to seal your position with an agent or editor, find a professional to collaborate with you who would lend his or her name to your book—and maybe even help you write it.

Senior agent Ellen Geiger represented the book *Body RX* by Dr. Scott Connelly and Carol Colman. "Connelly's company initially sent me a press kit and videotape. Typically, I will sign up a high-profile person like Connelly and then go looking for a writer. At the same time I was starting to look for a collaborator for Connelly, Carol Colman had contacted him independently for a piece she was writing. They clicked. Connelly himself suggested her, which is the best way. And the rest was easy. The sale [to Putnam in the fall of 2001] was in the seven figures.

"The lesson here is that when an author thinks he can write the book himself, he should think again! Getting the right collaborator can make all the difference. In this case, Connelly was an expert with no publishing experience. Colman was a trusted collaborator who not only wrote well, but also made the publishers feel comfortable because of her track record."

What Can Nonexperts Write About?

For many types of nonfiction, other than academic topics or health and psychology, only good research and writing skills are required. Agent Jessica Faust says, "If an author has a different spin on an old idea, he or she should probably be an expert. However, if an author has come up with a revolutionary idea, the idea can often be sold without the author being an expert."

Agent Dorian Karchmar also has hope to offer nonexpert nonfiction writers. "For certain kinds of nonfiction that are really about telling a story—nonfiction that reads like fiction—the question of expertise is a little less pertinent and varies on a case-by-case basis. In other words, for nonfiction that's really about the writing itself as much as it is about the subject matter, the credits that become important are the sorts of things agents and editors look for when they look at fiction: literary magazine publications, awards, workshops, and so on—rather than degrees and professional affiliations and the like."

Wise Words

I am always interested in why young people become writers, and from talking with many I have concluded that most do not want to be writers working eight and ten hours a day and accomplishing little; they want to have been writers, garnering the rewards of having completed a bestseller. They aspire to the rewards of writing but not to the travail.

—James Michener

How to Approach Agents and Editors

"Publishers are always on the lookout for a good book. This is something to keep in mind no matter how discouraging the prospect of finding a publisher is, no matter how many rejection slips you get, and no matter how overwhelming the odds seem."

—Richard Balkin

YOU'VE FOUND AND defined your book idea, targeted publishers or agents, and followed the advice in the earlier chapters. Now it's time to approach editors or agents with your idea. Remember, you're going to sell first, then write the book later.

Can I Really Sell the Book Before I Write It?

It's hard to believe, isn't it? Fiction writers know they must have a completed manuscript before even approaching editors or agents. Is it really possible to come up with a nonfiction book idea and not have to write the book if it doesn't fly? More than possible—it's the way you should approach getting your book published.

As mentioned in the Preface, most editors prefer to be able to help shape a book idea into a saleable product. "We buy books based on a proposal," says Contemporary Books editor Denise Betts. "I don't mind if the writer has written the book already, because then I know exactly what I'm getting and the process can move ahead more quickly, but from a writer's perspective, I wouldn't recommend it. The book may never see the printed page and the writer will have wasted much valuable time. Editors frequently buy projects based on a proposal, including a detailed table of contents and book outline, so writers will not be hindering their chances of getting published by approaching editors in this fashion."

Now let's hear what the agents have to say. They're the ones who regularly approach publishers and sell nonfiction books.

Anne Hawkins

"Most nonfiction can be sold on the basis of a proposal. The great exception is a memoir or autobiography by an author with no prior publishing credentials. That can be almost as difficult as selling a first novel with only a partial manuscript in hand."

Jessica Faust

"Some nonfiction can be sold based on a proposal. I would not recommend it with memoirs, however. But if you have an original idea and outstanding credentials, a sale based on the proposal is possible."

Ellen Geiger

"A good proposal is all that's required. In fact, I think it's frequently preferable because it makes less reading for the overworked editor who has to sift through an enormous pile of submissions every day."

If you send your query letter to too many agents, then receive some feedback that leads you to revise your idea, you'll have no one left to query. If you query too many editors first without luck, then find an agent, he or she won't have anyone left to whom to submit your material. Contact only five or six people at a time.

Dorian Karchmar

"I actually think the author is better off not having the manuscript completed. Editors who acquire the work often like to have some hand in helping to shape it. I always tell nonfiction writers to remember they are writing a proposal, not a book (though they will most likely need one or two sample chapters to go along with the proposal at the time of submission)."

Getting a proposal accepted has a usual progression of steps. Although there are exceptions, most follow this order:

1. You compose a stellar one-page query letter and send it, along with your self-addressed, stamped envelope (SASE), to five or six agents (or editors) at a time. At the bottom of the query letter you offer to send your full proposal on request.
2. A few requests trickle in. (Perhaps you also receive a few polite turndowns. These you keep note of in a submission log. You don't want to approach the same editor or agent twice with the same project by mistake. See suggestions for keeping track of your submissions later in this chapter.)
3. You make sure your proposal is professionally executed, and you send it off with a cover letter and another SASE. At this point, the number of possible scenarios broadens:

   • An agent or editor could call, E-mail, or write you and ask to see more—sample chapters, perhaps, and in some instances, the complete manuscript. Of course, you have not completed the manuscript and you make that clear. Your goal here is to sell your idea based on your proposal, then write the book.

- An agent could call, E-mail, or write you and offer to represent you.
- An editor could call, E-mail, or write you and offer to send you a contract.
- An agent or editor could send you a polite note of rejection. The reasons for declining could range anywhere from "Now that I've seen the full proposal, I realize the project won't sell" to "We've already done something like that," "The focus is too broad/narrow," or—least helpful—the simple "Not for us" turndown.

What do you do then? Keep sending out your query letters, or use the feedback you've received and go back and refine your idea. Find a different angle, a tighter focus, or a broader one. Look for more experts to quote, do more research, do more tweaking—whatever it takes.

There is something else to look at, though; the idea might be fine, but your writing skills might need some honing. Sometimes the idea is a killer, but the writing is not up to standard. There's no point in rushing to query and send out proposals before your writing is ready for the market. Try taking a writing course to get some professional feedback.

The last option is to shelve this idea and go on to the next. After all, the point of querying first is to see whether there's any interest. If not, you've saved yourself a lot of time and work.

How an Agent Sells Your Book Idea

Agents can approach editors in a couple of ways. Some will get on the phone and call, checking for initial interest before sending out any more material. Others will prepare a cover letter to go along with your proposal, then send out your package to editors they've identified as possible markets.

Agent Dorian Karchmar explains the process she went through for one particular book, starting with what she received from the writer and how she approached editors with it:

> I received a query from Roger Goldberg, a Harvard-trained surgeon working at Northwestern Medical Center in Chicago, for a book about the after-effects of pregnancy and labor on the female body, and what can be done to

avoid or ameliorate these symptoms. I requested the proposal, which he promptly supplied. The writing was strong, his credentials were solid, and though I regretted he didn't have a more developed platform with which to promote the book—a lecture series, workshops, his own radio show, and so on—the proposal was extremely thorough and professionally done.

But I didn't feel the proposal was focused correctly. He was trying to market it both to older women, who through menopause might be starting to experience certain problems caused by childbirth decades earlier, and also to young expectant mothers. I felt the divided focus would weaken the presentation—not least because it would be difficult to know where in the bookstore it would go—Childbirth? Menopause? So we worked together to figure out what the ideal focus would be. We decided it should be geared toward that broad swath of women of childbearing years, rather than fifty-plus baby boomers, as it was originally positioned.

I was also concerned that this have a clear hook beyond "another book about incontinence," and we came up with the title *Ever Since I Had My Baby*—because the key here is that this is the first definitive book about the linkage between childbirth and certain conditions such as incontinence.

The author reworked the material to reflect the focus, made ten copies of the proposal, and sent them to me. I made a list of editors specializing in women's health and medical issues and made my calls to pitch them the project—which was, by this time, very easy to pitch because we'd come up with a good title and a focused proposal.

Everyone wanted to see it. I ended up getting an offer from Crown just a few days after sending it out. It wasn't glitzy; it didn't make anyone rich; but it was a solid, easy sale!

You will find a copy of Roger Goldberg's query letter and book proposal in Chapter 4. You'll find the cover letter Dorian Karchmar prepared and sent out to prospective publishers with the proposal on pages 38–39.

Although, as mentioned earlier, selling nonfiction doesn't always require the services of an agent, this scenario shows clearly how an agent can be an invaluable ally. He or she can help you shape and focus your idea and then find the right editors to whom to deliver the pitch. An experienced agent can help close a deal that an inexperienced writer might not know how to pursue.

What Happens Once Your Idea Lands on an Editor's Desk

Editors receive unsolicited and solicited proposals; some are submitted by agents, some are submitted by writers. Seldom can one editor make a deci-

Dear _____,

As promised, I'm so pleased to enclose this
proposal for *Ever Since I Had My Baby* by the
wonderful Roger Goldberg, M.D., M.P.H., a Harvard-
trained specialist in reconstructive pelvic
surgery and urogynecology at Northwestern
University Medical School, with a master's in
public health from Johns Hopkins.

Ever Since I Had My Baby will be the first book
to explicitly address the most common physical
aftereffects of labor and delivery on a woman's
body—incontinence, prolapse, decreased sexual
satisfaction, and other conditions that result
from the weakening of the pelvic floor—and offer a
full spectrum of strategies for treating and even
preventing them.

The time is ripe for this guide. The NIH recently
voted to grant $10 million to the study of pelvic
floor disorders, and, as Dr. Goldberg writes,
"though only yesterday they were little spoken
of, the female conditions triggered by childbirth
account today for one of the most rapidly growing
medical and surgical subspecialties, and one of
the 'hottest' items on the national women's
health agenda." And Roger Goldberg, an associate
at one of the nation's leading centers for gynecological surgery, who publishes and lectures
widely internationally (c.v. enclosed), approaches this complex, delicate subject just as

one would wish: with unerring humor, clarity, and reassurance.

Ever Since I Had My Baby is not "just another incontinence book." Incontinence is, certainly, one important and common side effect of vaginal delivery. As is prolapse. As is—altogether too often—diminished sexual satisfaction. All of the above and more will be addressed fully in these pages. But what's exciting to me about *Ever Since I Had My Baby* is that it will be the first book on the shelf to "connect the disconnect between childbirth and pelvic floor injury—indeed between obstetrics and gynecology."

I hope you will find this proposal as timely and convincing as I clearly do. I'll be calling early next week to make sure you received this and hear your initial reaction.

All best,
Dorian Karchmar
Dorian Karchmar

sion to contract a book. The editor who first gets behind the book idea must convince coworkers in-house that the book is a viable project. The process varies from house to house. Some have two or three editors who must agree. Some must also convince a sales staff.

The following is a step-by-step look at a typical scenario for a book proposal. Keep in mind that this is only a general account of the process and it will vary from house to house.

1. The editor receives a query from the writer (or the writer's agent) and likes the idea.
2. The editor contacts the writer (or agent) and asks for the full proposal.
3. The editor sees the full proposal and wants to go ahead with the book.
4. The editor may or may not call the writer (or agent) to tell him or her that the proposal will be presented to the editorial board at their weekly meeting. (The editor may wait to make sure there is in-house interest before contacting the writer or agent. Or the editor will call first to make sure the writer has not contracted with another house.)
5. The editor might feel that the proposal is, in general, a solid one but that it may need some changes. He or she might suggest changes to the content or structure. (If too much reworking is required, the editor might decide not to pursue it because he or she will have too much to do to develop the project. The proposal must be very well thought out.)
6. The editor calls the writer (or agent) to talk about possible changes and determine whether the writer is agreeable to them.
7. If the writer is agreeable, the editor will circulate the proposal to the editorial board with a cover letter he or she has prepared pitching the book. The cover letter usually includes the idea's key points and why the editor feels his or her house should publish the book.
8. During the editorial board meeting, the group—usually consisting of representatives from the editorial, sales, marketing, and possibly publicity departments—discuss the position of the book in relation to the other books on their list, sales viability, and how much the project might cost.

An editor who likes your idea is more likely to call or E-mail you than use your SASE. Although you still must include that envelope, make sure you also include your phone number and your E-mail address in your query's letterhead and on the cover page of your proposal.

9. If the idea is approved in this meeting, sales figures are estimated and the advance is discussed. The details of the offer will be worked out and approved by the publisher before it is made to the author.
10. The editor informs the writer (or agent) of the publisher's interest and makes an offer.
11. The contract is drawn up and sent to the writer (or agent).
12. Once the writer (or agent) approves the contract, signs it, and sends back the signed copies, a check (usually for half the advance, depending on the terms negotiated) is issued and sent to the writer (or agent). See Chapter 5 for more information on contracts.
13. The writer begins work on the project.

Tools of the Trade

Let's back up a bit now and look at the pieces of paper you'll need to produce to get the attention of an agent or editor. The tools of the trade for the non-fiction writer include:

- Query letters
- Book proposals and all their elements
- Cover letters
- Follow-up letters
- Completed manuscripts

Let's not ignore one other tool, although this one is expressed verbally rather than through the written word. It's called a pitch line, and we'll go over that a little later in this chapter.

Query Letters That Grab Attention

The first step in this process is to compose a stellar query letter, which is a miniproposal with a twofold function. One is to gauge interest in your book idea. No point writing a book or working on a full proposal, if the reception you receive is on the tepid side. (Of course, you had to gather all the research for your proposal so you could successfully write the query—there are very few shortcuts in publishing.)

The other function of the query letter is to hook interest and get the editor or agent to ask to see more. Agent Wendy Sherman says, "I've read query letters that were just so interesting and intriguing that I called instantly and said, 'Please send it to me.' I'm sure there were others where the book was great, but I never got to it because the letter was just not intriguing enough. And, let's face it, we're talking about writing. Writing a letter is part of it."

"An engaging query letter is a thing of beauty," says senior agent Ellen Geiger, "guaranteed to get my attention instantly."

The best query letters are limited to one page. Some agents and editors even prefer just a couple of paragraphs. In this business, less is more. Learn to write tightly and avoid rambling. Leave plenty of white space on the page. The more quickly you get to the point, the more busy editors and agents will appreciate your approach.

Make sure your query letter is formatted like a professional business letter. Include your name, address, phone number, and E-mail address in your letterhead. "I hate reading a query letter that I love and there's no phone number or E-mail," says agent Simon Lipskar. "I have to send a letter back. It drives me crazy. I want to call them right away to tell them how much I loved their material and want to read more."

Single-space your one-page query letter. Put all paragraphs, including salutation, date, addresses, and sign-off, flush left, with an extra space between paragraphs. Alternatively, you can indent each paragraph with no extra space, but the flush left format looks a little neater and less cramped.

Address your query letter to a specific agent or editor. "Dear Sir or Madam" will not suffice. Double-check the spelling of all names; it doesn't hurt to check the gender, either. Agent Rob Cohen, for example, probably doesn't appreciate the "Dear Mr. Cohen" letters that come to *her* mailbox.

Agent Anne Hawkins says, "I like to receive a query first, then request the proposal if the project appears to be a good fit for my interests and editorial

> Write your query letter in the first person.

contacts. The two most important elements to me in a query letter are a clear, concise description of the project and the author's credentials for writing it."

Agent Nancy Abramson (Sedgeband Literary Associates) notes, "We pay particular attention to the writing skills within the query, and we do treat this as a résumé. Also, keep the query letter to one page."

Agent Wendy Sherman says a query letter should be just a couple of paragraphs: "Describe what your book is about, why you're writing it, and who you are."

What Ellen Geiger likes to see in a query letter is "a few paragraphs about the subject and its importance. One paragraph about the author's qualifications. No misspellings or obvious grammatical errors!"

Query Letter Checklist

Query letters must contain specific information. Use the following as a checklist:

- Concise, pithy description of the project
- The book's category (self-help, how-to, health, and so on)
- An estimated word count
- A brief rationale for your book, showing you've done your market research and found a gap in the marketplace
- The reason you're writing the book
- Significant details about your credentials
- Other credits, such as previous publications, awards won, and articles/stories published
- Your platform (possible promotional/publicity contacts)

> Do not confuse the word *titled* with the word *entitled*. **This book is titled**
> *How to Sell, Then Write Your Nonfiction Book*. *Entitled* **means something**
> **else: deserving, favored, privileged, permitted, and so on. These words are**
> **not the same.**

Query Letter Openings

It's perfectly acceptable to start your query letter with the formal approach: "I am seeking representation [when writing to an agent]/publication [when writing to an editor] for my proposed book, [insert title]."

It's acceptable, but boring. So many people start that way, it's in your favor to be more creative. Remember, the exercise here is to grab attention right away. That means you don't have the luxury to build up to anything. You must jump right in. Start with a brief anecdote or an interesting statistic. Find some piece of information that will intrigue and command interest. That's your hook.

It's also fine to start your query with a summary statement, giving an overview of your book: "My proposed book takes a nostalgic look at the period of time from 1950 to 1959" or "My proposed book is a survival manual for parents, covering how to cope with their teenager's sexuality." You could also start by giving the agent or editor a "handle" on your project. Your book is a cross between *The Zone* and Dr. Atkins. Or your book combines the suspense of *The Hot Zone* with the elements of Judith Miller's *Germs: Biological Weapons and America's Secret War*.

Although you should avoid using any adjectives in your query letter (see the sidebar on pages 46–47 for guidelines on what not to say in your query letter), you can make comparisons so the agents or editors will get a clear understanding of your book right up front.

Another way to start a query letter is with a referral—if you have one. Perhaps you met a published writer at a conference and she's suggesting you contact her editor. Or your neighbor, best friend, second cousin, or former father-in-law is a famous author and doesn't mind your mentioning that. Don't be afraid to name-drop when necessary.

> If your book fits an existing series in a publisher's catalog, make sure to mention that in your query letter.

The Body of the Query Letter

After your opening, compose another paragraph or two providing more information about your proposed book. Explain the purpose of the book, its subject matter, who the audience is, how you approach the topic, and any unusual formatting (the expected look of the finished product, types of photos, sidebars and text boxes, and so on). Be sure to state a rationale for your book, and reveal important details of the market analysis you conducted. If your book is the only one of its kind, say so. If your book focuses on an angle the other books have ignored, say so.

The last paragraph in your query letter before your sign-off is the author bio. Here you must make a case for why you're the best person to be writing the book you're proposing. That it's your idea isn't enough. Include your credits and credentials, any professional expertise you possess, any collaborators or experts willing to lend their name to your project. If you have a way to help promote the book—an extensive mailing list, fans from your TV program—then mention that, too. Although you don't want to brag or make grandiose statements, this is not the time to modestly fade into the wallpaper. Toot your own horn; no one else will.

> Always remember to include a #10 business-size SASE with your query letter. Fold it in thirds and make sure the flap is arranged so the glue won't accidentally seal itself. Put your address as the return address, not the editor's or agent's; if the SASE goes astray, you want it returned to you, not to the editor or agent.

Proposing a Series

If the book idea you have in mind could or should be part of a series, mention that in your query before the author bio and also in your proposal at the end of the overview section. Say something along the lines of "My proposed book could be the first of a series. I envision three additional books covering, x, y, and z." Make it brief and to the point. Don't go into any detail other than a quick overview of the other books.

What's especially important when proposing a series is to make sure you are querying about Book 1 of that series. If you query about Book 2 or 3, editors or agents will assume you had no luck proposing Book 1, and this will stymie any interest they might have had.

If your proposed book could also be a stand-alone book, make that clear as well. Some publishers are open to series. Others are not.

Closing Your Query Letter

Close your query letter with one simple line: "May I send you my full proposal?" No need to say thank you, no need to ask them to respond. No need to point their attention to the SASE you've enclosed. They'll assume that you'd like to hear their reaction and that you look forward to their response. They'll notice the SASE on their own. Don't fill up your query with unnecessary chitchat.

Query Letter Do's and Don'ts

Let's face it—writers without experience in the world of publishing can make mistakes. This checklist will help make sure your query is as error-free as possible.

- Do not admit this is your first book. That will be obvious if you have no credits to include.
- Do not include any negative information. That you got turned down by ten other agents, for example, won't endear any others to your project. Your desperation over your financial situation is not of interest, so leave that out. Sympathy won't gain you representation or a book contract—only good writing on a good project will.

- Do not discuss possible advances or royalty percentages at this point. It's way too early.
- Do not use any adjectives to describe your book. You're not writing book jacket blurbs here. Let the book reviewers rave about your book after it's out. Now is the time to let the writing speak for itself. The agent or editor will decide whether it's funny or informative, fast-paced or intelligently written.
- Do not tell the agent or editor that your book is destined to be a bestseller. No one can predict that.
- Do not insist they get back to you right away. Impatience isn't an attractive quality.
- Do use your computer's spellcheck tool, then double-check word for word for spelling errors. Spellcheckers won't know you meant "their" when you wrote "they're."
- Do make sure your grammar is correct. When in doubt, use a style guide.
- Do remember to include an SASE with your query letter.
- Do not send money or gifts or resort to other gimmicks.
- Do not fax your query.
- If you have permission to E-mail a query, do not send any attachments.
- Do not send your query letters (or proposals or completed manuscripts) registered or certified mail. Avoid making agents and editors run to the post office to sign for your mail.

Shortcuts to an Agent's or Editor's Ear

Why don't I just pick up the phone? you might be wondering. It would be a lot faster that way. Or just drop by. Get the agent's or editor's ear for ten minutes or so and tell them about my book idea. I could find out whether there's interest right away, and then I could forget about the query letter and send them the proposal—or go on to the next person on my list. Good idea?

> In your query letter and your proposal, write about your book in the
> future tense. "My book *will* cover _____" instead of "My book
> covers _____."

No. There are probably a million or so other unpublished writers thinking along the same lines as you. If agents and editors allowed it, they would spend their time doing nothing other than listening to book ideas on the phone. Most agents and editors will not accept phone calls from new writers.

There are always exceptions to the rule. If you're a multipublished writer, you might get by with a phone call. Some agents and editors expect that and even invite the contact. (Who would turn down a phone call from David McCullough? Maybe he needs a new agent or wants to switch publishing houses.) Or if you landed a contract on your own and are now shopping for an agent to negotiate the best deal for you and time is of the essence, your phone call will most likely be accepted.

If these two scenarios aren't the case for you, though, and you'd still like to find a way to talk to an editor or agent, try attending a writers' conference—that would be your best bet. Most writers' conferences give attendees the option to sign up for a ten- to fifteen-minute agent/editor appointment. Most conferences do not charge extra for this service. (Some do, but this is frowned upon by the Association of Authors' Representatives.)

How many agents and editors you'll be able to see will depend on the conference (usually one or two is the norm) and how assertive you are. There's certainly nothing wrong with pitching to an agent you're seated next to at dinner or rubbing elbows with in the conference hall, lobby, or hotel bar. Be judicious, though. Don't get so eager that you follow agents and editors into the restrooms.

During the assigned appointment you'll be able to pitch your book idea. In advance of this appointment, you'll want to prepare your pitch line, a short sentence that conveys the subject matter of your proposed book in a compelling way. Make sure to state the genre and subgenre, if there is one. Many of the agents and some of the editors handle both nonfiction and fiction. Let them know up front into which arena your book falls. For example, your nonfiction book is a travel guide.

Do not drop by an editor's or agent's office unannounced. "Every day we have people who call or drop by and want to meet with us on the spur of the moment," says agent Frances Kuffel (Jean Naggar Literary Agency). "They don't realize how busy and scheduled our lives are. They are often abrupt, demanding, and condescending. Don't they realize that the people concerned are going to weigh that in, whether they're going to take a person on as a client or whether they're going to stick with someone when things get bad? It would be hilarious if it weren't such a trial."

The agent or editor will ask you questions—probably more about your book idea and your qualifications—and you'll have a give-and-take discussion. By the end of your time, if the agent or editor is hooked, he or she will ask to see more. That means you have bypassed the query stage and will be sending him or her your proposal and maybe a sample chapter or two. You'll also send a cover letter along with this package. More on cover letters later in this chapter.

For some new writers, the thought of meeting face to face with an editor or agent can be daunting. Keep in mind that editors and agents are people, too. Some are friendly and confident and will immediately make you feel at ease. Others are more comfortable with manuscripts than the masses. You'll have to put them at ease.

The editor or agent might also be young and new to the field. This happens more than you realize. The new graduates are the ones who more often than not attend conferences. They haven't had time yet to build up their stables—what better place to find new talent than at a writers' conference. But because they're young and inexperienced, they might be even more nervous about this than you are! Relax and help them to relax. And read the do's and don'ts list on pages 50–52 to get the most out of your agent/editor appointment.

The Elements of a Book Proposal

It's important that your query letter be the best writing you produce. If it isn't, you won't easily get to this step—sending in your book proposal. And that's

Preparing Yourself for That Ten-Minute Agent/Editor Appointment

Do's

- Make sure you know how to find the room so you'll be on time.

- Dress appropriately (avoid lots of jewelry, perfume, or aftershave).

- Take a deep breath, smile, shake hands, and introduce yourself.

- If you're really nervous and you don't know where to begin, tell the agent/editor that. It will help break the ice and he or she will probably give you a clue or ask you a question.

- Tell the agent/editor what your project is. Get right to the point and deliver your pitch. (You can say you have prepared a pitch line—would he or she like to hear it?)

- Then stop talking for a moment—let the agent/editor ask you some questions.

- Prepare in advance for questions you might be asked and have your answers ready.

- If the agent/editor expresses interest, make sure you ask what specific material he or she would like you to send (sample chapters, proposals, outlines).

- If the agent/editor has asked for more material, make sure to give him or her your business card—and write the name of your project on the back of it.

- Also get the agent's/editor's business card so you know where to send the requested material and how to spell his or her name. Write down what he or she has asked to see so you don't forget.

- If the agent/editor says he or she isn't interested, thank him or her for any feedback provided. You can also ask if he or she could suggest anyone else for you to approach.

- Be aware of the time. When your time is up, say thank you and leave. (Even if the agent/editor seems to want to continue beyond the time, remember there are other writers waiting.)

- After the meeting, send your material with a cover letter, reminding the agent/editor where you met, giving a brief recap of your project—you can use your pitch here, too—and that the material was solicited.

Don'ts

- Do not bring your manuscript, proposal, outline, query, or any other material (except a business card) to the appointment. Agents/editors generally don't have time to read during the appointment or the conference. They will ask you to send material to their office after the conference. The exception to this is if you've had a related book published; bring that along to show them.

- Don't be late for the appointment. If you are late, don't expect the agent/editor to squeeze you in. That makes other writers late.

- Don't hog the whole ten minutes. Make sure the agent/editor has time to speak.

- Don't gush or tell him or her how wonderful your project is or that it will be the next bestseller. Leave the adjectives for the reviewers and the predictions for the psychics.

- Don't digress. Stay on the subject of your project(s).

- Don't make an appointment if you don't have a specific project to discuss. This isn't the time or place to pick an agent's/editor's brains about the publishing world in general.

- Don't ask agents questions about how they work or editors about how they will promote you or how much they'll pay you. These types of questions are asked only when you've been offered representation or a publishing contract.

- Don't ask why if the agent/editor says he or she isn't interested. It just puts him or her on the spot.

- If the agent/editor asks to see more, don't push for a time frame for a response.

- If you are asked to send material, don't call or write to see if the agent/editor has received it or has an answer yet. Allow three to six months or more before sending a follow-up letter. Agents and editors are notoriously swamped after conferences and often get way behind with their reading.

- Don't burn any bridges! You never know when you might have the opportunity to approach these people again. Let them remember you as the pleasant writer, not the pushy, difficult one.

what all your research and enthusiasm have been geared toward—presenting your book idea in a way that will land you a contract based on your proposal. But the query letter isn't the only item that must be professional and polished—your proposal must be as well. And if it hits its mark, you'll see a contract come sailing back to you in your SASE.

Agent Dorian Karchmar says, "Write a proposal that anticipates an agent's/editor's questions and doubts and lays them to rest. This means knowing your subject; knowing your market; and understanding who your audience is, why they are going to want to buy your book rather than the other four books out there on the same subject, and why you're the best person to write the book.

"The goal of the proposal is to organize all your ammunition into a readable and hyperconvincing package. Remember, the bottom line is to convince anyone who reads the proposal not just that the book is worthy of publication, but that it will sell (that lots of people will buy it). Know your market."

Agent Jessica Faust advises, "Because you aren't able to present an editor with all the material—the full manuscript—it is essential to make sure the material you are submitting—the proposal—is well written, complete, and concise."

"The best nonfiction proposals are by writers who have a deep understanding of their subject and preferably some degree of quantifiable authority in the area," adds agent Richard Henshaw. "Obviously the proposals have to be written in an appropriate and/or accessible style. The authors should know the competition in their chosen area and be able to argue convincingly that their book can compete with other works in the market."

"I appreciate well-crafted and thought-out proposals," says editor Denise Betts. "These stand apart from the rest and are more likely to garner a favorable response because the benefits of the book and the need for it will be obvious straightaway. Make the proposal easy for the editor to read and navigate. Editors' time is limited, so you don't want to bog them down with italics and various crazy fonts."

Every project is different and needs to be described differently, but most successful proposals contain the following elements:

Title or cover page
Table of contents (for the proposal)
Introduction/overview
Audience/market for the book
Competitive/comparative titles
Format
Author biography
Publicity and promotion
Sample table of contents (for the proposed book)
Chapter summaries/chapter outline
Sample chapter
Resources needed to complete the book
Delivery
Supplementary materials

Let's have a look at each one in the order they will be featured in your proposal:

Title or Cover Page

In the upper left corner of the title page, list your name, address, phone number, and E-mail address. Centered in the middle of the page, type

```
Book Proposal:

[Your Proposed Book's Title]

by [Your Name]
```

The title page should not be numbered and should contain no fancy fonts, although you can use bold to highlight the proposed book's title.

Now that we're at the title page, it would be a good time to discuss your book's title. As agent Dorian Karchmar mentioned earlier in this chapter, a good title helps an agent pitch your work more effectively. It also helps you pitch your work to prospective agents or editors. Editor Denise Betts agrees: "Have a well-thought-out title. Don't get too creative or esoteric. Keep to the thrust or hook of the book. Often a project will have a mark against it simply because the title is off-putting, doesn't immediately convey what the project is about, or just simply isn't working."

When planning your title, try to use as few words as possible. If those few words don't convey the thrust of your book, you can always add a more explanatory subtitle.

Don't get too attached to your title, however. Could be it's already in use or there's some other reason to change it. Many times editors have their own ideas on what your book should be called and will discuss that with you.

Table of Contents (for the Proposal)

Your proposal will have two tables of contents. Later in the proposal you'll feature the contents page for your proposed book, but the first table of contents you'll include will give agents and editors an idea of what the proposal itself contains. It comes directly after the title page and will look something like this:

Proposal Table of Contents

1.	Introduction	1
2.	The Market	5
3.	Competing Titles	8
4.	Format	9
5.	Author Bio	10
6.	Publicity and Promotion	12
7.	Supplemental Materials	15
8.	Sample Table of Contents	15
9.	Chapter Summaries	17
10.	Sample Chapter	25

Although your proposal's contents will come first, directly after the title page, you'll fill in the page numbers after you're finished writing the proposal.

The order in which you include the various elements can vary. For example, sometimes you'll provide your supplemental materials separate from the proposal, especially if you have photocopied newspaper clippings or are including illustrations. (More on illustrations under Format.) Or you might want to mention competing or comparative titles earlier to highlight the importance of your book.

Introduction/Overview

Your introduction or overview should provide a concise statement of your proposed book's concept, content, and purpose. Here you can reuse the opening paragraph or two of your query letter with its refined pitch line, handle, or hook. (Unlike the query letter, however, your proposal's introduction is not the place for name-dropping.)

Include relevant anecdotes in this section. You can also include any statistics or quotes from experts.

Make sure the overview is organized logically, with one thought flowing into the next and transitions to tie each paragraph together. Be careful not to jump from one thought to the next. Decide what you'll cover first, second, and so on. Some writers find it helpful to make an outline or list the points they want to include in the overview section, then refer to that outline or list as they write. You have a lot of information you're juggling and you don't want to forget anything or include something in the wrong place.

Remember to refer to your book as your *proposed* book, even if you've already written it.

The tone and style of your overview—in fact, of your entire proposal— should reflect the tone and style you'll be using in your book. If the book will have a chatty style, for example, then your proposal can be chatty, too.

Audience/Market for the Book

In this context the audience for your book is also referred to as its market. Who's going to buy and read your book? This is not the place to brag that every man, woman, and child will be a fan of your book. In fact, in many cases, the narrower your audience, the easier they are to reach and the happier you'll make publishers. A book geared to all men, for example, will not be as easy to market

> With some clever editing, the overview you compose for this proposal
> could be restructured and used as the introduction of your book. See
> more on that in Chapter 6.

as a book geared toward men over fifty. This is because the publisher's publicity and sales departments can more easily reach a specific group.

"Be realistic and optimistic," says editor Denise Betts. "Do not overin-
flate the audience for the book or its salability. For example, if you're pitching a book on changing careers, do not cite hundreds of thousands of baby
boomers as your audience. It's too broad, rings hollow, and takes away credibility from your project. If your audience is a small niche, but there's currently no other resource for them to turn to, then your project has more of
a chance than if it's a large audience and the area has been overpublished. Do
a detailed and well-researched competitive analysis. This saves the editor a lot
of time and will speed your proposal through the acquisitions process."

Ideally, you should have decided on your audience as you were defining
your book idea, before you even got to the proposal writing stage. But if your
book idea carried you away and the actual market for your book hasn't crossed
your mind yet, use the research you must do for this proposal to help you
define that. Sometimes writing a book proposal can help you see how mar-
ketable your idea will be—or not be.

Can't narrow down the market for your book? That might be a clue to
redefine your book idea. Make sure you are gearing this idea to a particular
audience. Always keep in mind who your readers are when writing a book.

Competitive/Comparative Titles

The research you do for this section of your proposal will also help you see
whether your book idea will fly or not. If you're finding too many competing titles—in fact, the market is flooded with books on your subject—then
it might be time to drop this idea and move on to something else. If there
are a few competing titles, but they don't cover the same material your book

does, this is important information for you to know—and important information for you to convey in your proposal.

It's not necessary to list every competing book. List a few that are most relevant—those that might cause the editors the most concern. Put their concerns at rest. Yes, there is a well-known bestseller on the subject, but your book is substantially different (or better) because it takes the subject one step further or focuses on one particular angle of that subject.

If there are no competing titles, make sure once again to calm skittish editors. It's not that there's no interest in your subject matter (remember my English cookbook mentioned in the Preface), it's just that your idea is so new and revolutionary, it hasn't been covered yet.

Format

In this section you include the projected word count of your proposed book, how the book will be organized, how many parts and/or chapters it will have, and how you'll approach each chapter. For example, will all chapters follow a similar format? If you plan to start each chapter of your self-help book with a brief case study and end each chapter with a self-assessment test, note that.

To estimate your finished book's word count, keeping in mind that word count will vary depending on the trim size of the book, first decide how many chapters you'll have. You'll do this when creating your sample table of contents. Perhaps your book lends itself to ten chapters. Because most chapters run 15 to 20 pages, you can take a number somewhere in between, such as 18. Multiply 18 by the number of chapters. That equals 180. The average number of words per page runs between 250 and 350. Use a number somewhere in between, such as 300. Multiply 300 by 180 and you've got a book whose estimated word count is 54,000.

Double-check the guidelines you've requested from publishers to make sure your estimated book length is in the appropriate range.

(This can also be noted in the chapter summaries section, discussed later in this chapter.)

The format section is also the place to mention other materials you plan to include in your book, such as photographs, charts, or drawings. Be specific. State that you envision ten color photographs and three charts for the entire book or that each chapter will need its own illustrations.

Remember that books with color photographs are expensive to produce and publishers might not be willing to go to such expense. Mention photographs as a possibility, but don't insist on them. Also, black-and-white photographs are less expensive and might be more appropriate to the kind of book you're proposing.

It will also help your case if you can provide the illustrations. (An exception to this is if you're proposing a book aimed toward children. Most publishers of children's books work with their own staff or favorite freelance illustrators.) If your plan is for a colorful coffee-table book, sending sample photos (or slides) along with your proposal isn't a bad idea. Sometimes photos can sell the work. Just make sure you send copies, not the originals.

Also mention in the format section what back matter the book will have—for example, appendices offering a list of recommended reading, professional associations, or other useful resources.

If you envision a special size for the book, mention that, too. Remember, though, that books too big (or too tiny) for library and bookstore shelves won't have as much chance of getting published as more traditional sizes. You can suggest the size you'd like to see and provide a rationale for a deviation from the norm, but don't insist on it.

Author Biography

In this section you must sell yourself as the best person to be writing this book. It isn't enough that you thought up the idea or even that you can write well. Your idea might be a winner, but if your credentials don't measure up, publishers might decide to opt out. Although, depending on the book, you don't always have to be an expert in the field (see Chapter 2), you do need some credentials or related experience to qualify as the best author for this particular book.

Look carefully at your proposed book's topic. If there's an obvious connection—for example, you have a Ph.D. in early childhood education and your book covers aspects of early childhood education—then say so. The

Agent Anne Hawkins says she prefers the author bio section to be written in the third person. "It's just one notch more professional. Third person allows the listing of the author's credentials and publications without sounding as though she is tooting her own horn. Silly, I know, because it's obvious that the author wrote the section, but that's the impression it gives."

related degree does qualify you. If your book is a layperson's approach to handling the terrible twos and you just happen to be the parent of twin two-year-olds, make that clear.

But if your book is a new approach to dog training and the only qualifications you have are a good idea and an impressive Doberman, you might need some extra help building your case. Do qualified dog trainers use your method? Do veterinarians endorse you? Will they provide you with quotes? Contact them and find out. Have you won an award from the professional association responsible for the field you're writing about? Will they endorse you? Have you been giving classes using your method? Will your students endorse you? Find as many ways as possible to build your case.

Include, of course, any prior publications, relevant academic or professional qualifications, articles written about you, or any public speaking you've done.

If you're having trouble coming up with reasons you'd be the best author for this book, you might have to think again about this particular topic. Remember, part of the purpose of the book proposal is to help you see whether you have a viable book idea. If you're not able to convince publishers you would be a believable author for this project, then there's no point in going further with it. Look for another topic for which you would be viewed as qualified or look for ways to build your credentials. Consider going back to school or entering some sort of related training program. Do what you need to do to sell yourself to publishers.

Publicity and Promotion

In the author bio section you sell yourself. In the publicity and promotion section you need to show how you could help sell the book if publishers went ahead and published it. This information further emphasizes the previous section. The *right* author for this book will have a platform from which to promote the book.

Platform is the word agents and editors use to describe the ways you can help sell a book. Let's go back to that dog trainer. He convinced the adult education center in his neighborhood to allow him to teach a course. He's been teaching that course for several semesters now and it's always full. There are a lot of dog owners who want to learn how to train their pets. He wisely made sure to keep a copy of the postal and E-mail addresses of all his former students. He could mail a flyer to all of them, or he could provide the list to the publisher. Not only can he contact former students, but also he has a slew of current and future students to reach. In fact, he can offer his book as a required text for anyone wanting to sign up.

He is also thinking ahead. He will hire a publicist to get him guest speaking engagements around the country. His method for training dogs is so effective that word of mouth has begun to spread and others want to learn about him. He'll offer the book as part of the enrollment fee.

Back on his home territory, he knows the owner of a local independent bookstore who would be happy to host a book signing. The local radio station manager would also be happy to help. He's envisioning a listener phone-in Q&A session.

Finally, this dog trainer/author knows HTML and he's putting up a website for himself. This will generate even more publicity for his proposed book.

If you don't have a platform, work to create one for yourself. Use a little imagination, and you'll figure out a way to promote yourself. A platform can consist of any or all of the following:

- You have a mailing list or know how to build one.
- You have a website.
- You teach workshops or classes.
- You have your own radio show or access to one.
- You own your own bookstore.
- You have a following you can document, an audience you can reach.

What if you don't have a platform? Other than your willingness to tour the country for book signings and be a guest on Letterman or Leno (which you will not mention—all writers dream of this; few achieve it), you have no means to promote the book. If that's the case, then eliminate this section from your proposal. There's no need to point out a negative. Including the heading and then admitting you have nothing to say in this area will be less helpful than completely omitting the mention of it. Agents and editors either will assume you neglected to mention your platform (they'll probably ask you about it) or will figure out from your author biography section that you don't have one. This won't break a book deal, although having a healthy platform could help make the deal. In any event, make sure the rest of your proposal is solid. See Chapter 7 for more information on publicity and promotion.

Sample Table of Contents (for the Proposed Book)

The format of the sample table of contents for your proposed book should look just like a real table of contents. Turn to the Contents of this book and use it as an example. The sample table of contents is a chance for you to show that you've carefully considered the material you'll cover and in what order you'll present it.

Make sure your chapters are laid out in logical order. Note under each chapter all key points you'll cover in that chapter. Don't worry, though. This table of contents is only a sample and not etched in stone. If you land a contract for the book and discover while writing it that it makes more sense to rearrange the order of the chapters or include or omit information, you can make changes then. You will need to discuss substantive changes from your original plan with your editor. There's always leeway when getting down to the actual writing. For more information on writing the actual book turn to Chapter 6.

Chapter Summaries/Chapter Outline

Seldom when you see the word *outline* in the publishing industry does it mean the type of ABC-123 outline you had to create in high school. In this context, a chapter outline is the same as a chapter summary—and can be handled in a number of ways.

Write your chapter summaries/outline in the present tense.

One approach is to write a brief narrative synopsis of the content of each chapter, providing a paragraph or two and hitting the salient points of each chapter. Make sure to vary your prose—avoid using the same structure for every sentence in each summary, and avoid overusing the same verbs. However, this approach can lead the agent or editor to feel your chapters might not have enough substance.

Try an outline approach without the ABCs. Use headings and subheadings. Make sure that instead of describing specifics from the proposed text, you state that the chapter describes the specifics. For example, in that English cookbook you would not explain the history of a dish; you would point out that you explain the history or origin of each dish in the chapter.

If each of your chapters is formatted exactly the same, then a simplified chapter summaries section will suffice. For example, you're proposing a travel guide and each chapter will cover a different city. Then under each chapter you'd just list:

Accommodations
Food
Attractions
Day trips
And so on

Rarely with fiction will you see chapter titles, but it is the norm with most nonfiction. Your titles can be straightforward, such as the chapter titles in this book. One quick glance at the table of contents and the reader knows what to expect.

Catchy titles can work, too. If you decide to be creative, make sure to give each chapter a subtitle so the content is clear.

Avoid the passive voice in your chapter summaries:

Say: The first part of Chapter 1 provides a history of each dish.

Do not say: A history of each dish is provided in the first part of Chapter 1.

Sample Chapters

Even though in many cases a new writer can, indeed, sell a book based on a proposal without writing the book first, some editors expect to see at least one sample chapter, if not more. The sample is to give them an idea of your writing style beyond what they see in the proposal and to show them how you approach the topic. The proposal sells the idea; the sample chapter or chapters can nail the contract.

Send the introduction to your book and at least the first chapter for this sample.

Resources Needed to Complete the Book

Some guides suggest you get out your calculator and figure out what your phone or photography or travel expenses would be—then include that in your proposal. This guide suggests you omit that section. Most editors don't need to read this in your proposal. If you're proposing a travel guide, for example, the editor will most likely tell you up front whether there would be any expense money available. If the house is interested and wants to go ahead with the project, you can negotiate for expenses in your contract (see Chapter 5). If you absolutely need a big chunk of money to finish the book and the publisher is unwilling or unable to provide that, you might have to go elsewhere—or shelve the project. There's not much point in proposing a book that will require a hefty budget. Publishers will shy away from that when working with a new writer. Wait until you have a track record before planning on an expense account.

Delivery

Some proposals include a short paragraph stating when you can deliver the manuscript. But for the most part, this is another section that isn't necessary.

In your proposal you are addressing editors and agents. In your sample chapters you are addressing future readers of your book. Avoid the pronoun *you* in your proposal, but feel free to use it in your sample chapters if appropriate.

If the book is already written and you can deliver the manuscript immediately, there's really no point to the proposal. Remember, this is a proposed book, not a completed one. You want to make sure the editor can feel he or she would have a part in the creation of the finished product.

If the book isn't written and you know you can write it in a month or two months—or you need a year because any day now you're expecting your first baby, going on an around-the-world cruise, or finishing up some other project—keep this to yourself until the time is right.

The time is right when the editor wants to go ahead with the book. Then you can discuss your schedule and any problems you might have. The editor can also explain what her needs are. She's filling out her line for the next season, or the season after that. When she expects the book to come out will determine how much time you get to write it. If you mention problems in the proposal, it might worry the editor out of making a positive decision on your book. Always be candid with editors about your time frame, but don't jump in too early with unnecessary information.

Supplementary Materials

You've just written a ten-, twenty-, maybe even a fifty-page proposal. What else could there be to say? The supplementary materials section includes materials that back up what you've asserted in your proposal. Supplementary materials are anything that will strengthen your case, such as published articles you've written or seen or articles written about you.

For example, in your overview for your proposed how-to book for new mothers juggling careers and babies, you cite statistics reporting that 78 percent of new mothers go back to their jobs within six weeks of giving birth. You found these statistics in a recent *New Mother* magazine article. The article backs up your claim that new mothers need help (and your proposed book would be just the help they need). The article lends credence to the viability of your book idea. Clip out that article, photocopy it, and attach it to your proposal package in the supplementary materials section.

Have you found magazine and newspaper articles that cry out for a book such as yours? Do they show the start of a trend? Do they back up your assertion? Did you jump and say hallelujah when you saw these articles? The editors might jump, too. Make sure to give them a reason. Collect whatever information is out there, including articles, photographs, and write-ups about popular TV shows covering your topic, or, if applicable, videotapes of a segment on *60 Minutes* or *20/20* or any other program related to your project. If you or your idea is getting attention, it's important to let agents and editors know about it.

Miniproposals

Occasionally, if you have an ongoing relationship with a publisher, you can avoid writing extensive proposals. You'll discuss the idea first with your editor, most likely over the phone or through an E-mail or two. The conversation might go something like this:

"I noticed in your catalog that you don't have a book on English cooking. You have a whole series, covering most of the countries of Europe, but none on the British Isles. Could I send you a proposal for an English (or Irish or Welsh or Scottish) cookbook?"

The editor will either tell you why there's no book in their line on that subject or say, "Yes, that's a good idea. Send me something." In the latter case the something you'd send would most likely be a few paragraphs to a page or so of an overview/introduction/rationale for the book and a sample table of contents.

The overview would differ slightly from a full-length proposal's overview. In a miniproposal you need to say in one or two pages what you might take ten pages to say in a full proposal. Your one- or two-page overview should include the following:

- **A few paragraphs introducing/explaining your book idea.** Get right to the crux of your book idea in the first sentence. Back it up with any statistics or anecdotes you've uncovered. Make the topic you'll cover clear.
- **A rationale for the book.** Just because there are no books on your idea in your publisher's catalog doesn't mean there aren't other similar books with other publishers. Make sure there's a need out there for this book. Editors seldom can make a solo decision to acquire a book. Other people are involved. So give your editor enough information that he or she can take to the committee meeting to sell your idea.
- **The market.** Let the editor know who would read this book. He or she can then figure out whether this is an audience your publisher knows how to reach.

- **An author biography section.** Put this in even if you think your editor knows you so well that she or he might know every skill or talent in your repertoire. Perhaps you have some experience related to this particular book topic. Maybe you lived in England for a number of years and that's where you learned all about English cooking. Make clear your special connection to the proposed book.

In addition to your overview, be sure to include a sample table of contents for your proposed book. List the chapters and what material each chapter will cover, obviously following a logical order. Just as with the full proposal, the table of contents in a miniproposal will give the editor a clear idea of what you plan to include.

Editors aren't the only ones to whom you would send a miniproposal. You might also be able to use this type of proposal if you have an ongoing relationship with an agent. After a pitch over the phone and the agent's go-ahead, a brief overview and table of contents will give her or him a sense of whether this is a book idea she or he could sell.

Cover Letters

Along with your full or miniproposal, you will send a cover letter. The difference between a cover letter and a query letter is this: whereas a query letter is a miniproposal and often your first contact with an editor or agent, a cover letter simply—well—*covers* what you were asked to send. Cover letters accompany solicited material. Their function is to remind the person you're writing who you are, how you met (for example, at a writers' conference or through your initial query letter), that your material was requested, and what your material is. Your one-sentence pitch line that you included in your query letter or used at the writers' conference (or over the phone with your editor or agent) will work well here.

Be sure to include a cover letter with your miniproposal package.

Sample Cover Letter

Your Name
Your Address
Your Phone Number
Your E-mail

Date

Agent's or Editor's Name, Title (if an editor)
Agency or Publishing House Name
Street Address
City, State, Zip

Dear [use Mr./Ms./Mrs. unless first name usage
has already been established]:

It was a pleasure meeting you last month at the
Southeast Writers Group Conference, held in
Atlanta. I hope you enjoyed the Friday night
speaker and banquet as much as I did.

I appreciated your taking time from dinner to
discuss my proposed book, *The English Good Food
Cook Book*, a collection of traditional English
recipes.

As I mentioned, I am a freelance writer with
articles in *Newsday*, *British Heritage*, *Fort
Lauderdale News/Sun-Sentinel*, *Gulf Air's
Inflight*, *What's On*, *International Living*,
Accent, *AAA Going Places*, *Horseplay*, *Coins*,

Mainstream, Sign Craft, and various other
publications.

At your suggestion, I have enclosed my proposal
and one sample chapter for *The English Good Food
Cook Book*.

I look forward to your reaction.

Sincerely,
Your signature
Your name typed

*Don't forget to enclose an SASE—a #10 business-size envelope for a response
only, or a 9 × 12 or larger for the return of your proposal.*

The cover letter should be formatted like a business letter and should also include your book's title and genre. If it's covering your proposal, make sure it draws attention to your book's hook and any other important facts you can present succinctly.

You might notice an agent or editor using the term *cover letter*, or you might see cover letters mentioned in a market guide, when what is really meant is *query letter*. Look for the context. The query letter is the first contact, suggesting a project and offering the full proposal. A cover letter accompanies solicited material.

If you decide to send your proposal or other material along with your one-page query letter as your first contact (even though the best initial contact is just the query), then the query serves a dual function: proposal and cover letter. It's proposing a project and covering material you're sending. Remember, though, that in this case your proposal is unsolicited. It's much better to query first and get the go-ahead. Then you can send your proposal with your cover letter, having confidence that this material was requested and will get full consideration.

Follow-Up Letters

You've sent off your material and you've been waiting eagerly for a response. Patience has never been your strong suit. You're dying to find out what's happening. You start composing a follow-up note, but you're not sure what to say. Before discussing what such a letter should include, let's first talk about when to follow up. Examine this chart:

Item	When to Follow Up
Unsolicited query letters	Never. You sent the query unsolicited. Don't expect an answer.
Solicited query letters	Never. There's really no such thing as a solicited query letter. If you're querying, it's because you haven't spoken to the agent or editor first and have not been asked to send any material.

Solicited proposals	Check the editor's guidelines or the market guides to see what time frame the editor or agent asks you to allow and then add a few weeks on top of that. It's usually at least four to eight weeks.
Unsolicited proposals	Never. There's no point in following up on something you sent without being asked.

From this chart you can see that you should send follow-up letters only for solicited material and that you need to wait a decent amount of time before following up. Showing your impatience and, even worse, harassing editors and agents will not win you any points.

When a respectable amount of time has passed and you haven't heard back, it is time to send a brief, polite note. The follow-up letter should be typed on your letterhead stationery, which should include your phone number and E-mail address. The note should say something simple and straightforward, such as the following. Make sure to include a #10 business-size SASE with your note.

```
Dear _____:


I am writing to follow up on my proposal for [fill in
the title of your book idea], which I sent to you at
your request on [fill in the date].

Could you please let me know its status?

Sincerely,

Your signature
Your name typed
```

Completed Manuscripts

If all goes well—your pitch or query letter is well received and you send in a fantastic proposal—you'll get that glorious approval to write a book

> Do not telephone an agent or editor to follow up on a query letter. "Writers have to recognize that agents are really busy," says agent Wendy Sherman, "and that we spend a lot of our time reading transom material, as well as doing our job, which is selling the material we already represent. A little patience and understanding is appreciated."

under contract (see Chapter 5). You must then complete the last stage of the getting-published process. You must write the manuscript. (You'll find help for researching, organizing, and actually writing your manuscript in Chapter 6.)

Formatting and Submission Details

Admittedly, what you have to say in your query letter, your proposal, and your cover letter is more important than the format you use—but only just. Agents and editors could easily miss what you have to say if it's presented in a way that makes it difficult to read.

For a successful approach to agents or editors follow these formatting guidelines:

Spacing

As a general rule, material that is one page long should be single-spaced, and anything longer than that must be double-spaced. So your one-page query letter and your one-page cover letter would be single-spaced; every page of your proposal, including the two contents pages, chapter summaries, and sample chapters, should be double-spaced.

Margins

Allow a one-inch to an inch-and-a-half margin all the way around. Do not justify the right margin; leave it ragged.

Font Type and Size

Use Times New Roman size 12 or Courier size 10. Avoid fancy fonts. Use bold sparingly and limit it to headings or subheadings. You can use underlining to indicate italics, or you can use the actual italics. Use italics only for foreign words or the titles of publications.

SASEs

Include a return envelope with every piece of correspondence until your book is under contract. That means that you send an SASE with your guidelines request, query letter, cover letter, proposal, and if necessary, follow-up letter. Agents or editors might never use your SASEs—and that's a good thing. Most acceptances come by telephone or even E-mail. But you must include them as a courtesy, in case your project isn't accepted.

Use a #10 business-size SASE for all one-page correspondence. If your proposal gets turned down and you want the agent or editor to return it, include an envelope that's large enough, such as a manila envelope folded once, with sufficient postage to cover the weight of your proposal and any additional correspondence the agent or editor might decide to send you. If you don't want the proposal back, send only the #10 business size.

Do not use metered postage. Do not send cash to cover the postage. Do not send loose stamps.

If you live outside the United States, send International Reply Coupons (IRCs). You can purchase these at most post offices around the world. There are exceptions to that, though. If you can't find IRCs where you live, have a friend in the States send you enough stamps. Make sure to find out the correct amount to cover the cost of mailing a rejection letter from America to your country. It is acceptable to use the lighter airmail envelopes for your SASEs.

Running Heads and Page Numbering

At the top of each page of your proposal beginning with your overview, have a line that looks like this:

```
Your Last Name/Proposal for Your Book's Title    page #
```

If your book title is more than a few words long, you might need to shorten it in the running head and use only the title's key words.

Most word processing programs have a header function, and that is what you should use. The header should be at the top of your pages, separated from your text by several line spaces. Use a similar running head for your sample chapters. Look at Chapter 6 of this book for manuscript formatting information.

Start numbering your proposal from the first page of your overview. Make that page one and then number all subsequent pages in the proposal consecutively. The exception to that rule is sample chapters. If you're including the introduction and/or first chapter, number those pieces separately from the proposal; each should begin with page one.

Packaging Your Proposal or Completed Manuscript

Make sure to submit your pages loose. Do not bind your proposal or your completed manuscript. Do not use a folder. For a large number of pages—more than a hundred or so—you can use a rubber band to hold things together. Large manuscripts can also be mailed in cardboard manuscript boxes, available at any office supply store. But loose is most often the preferred method.

Don't overwrap your submission. Using too much tape or staples makes the package difficult for editors or agents to open. This won't endear you to them, especially if a padded envelope tears and all that stuffing ends up covering their desk and carpet.

Never staple your pages together. Submit them loose or, if necessary, use paper clips to separate different sections of your package.

Don't resort to gimmicks—or bribery. A gift of chocolate, for example, especially if it melts all over your pages, also won't make you popular.

Use plain white paper. No ribbons. No perfume.

Keeping Track of Your Submissions

Staying organized is important in this business. You want to know where your query letters and proposals are, where they've been, and whom they're going out to next. If you have more than one project in the works, keeping track of all your submissions is even more important. You don't want to send the wrong proposal to the wrong agent or editor. And you don't want to resubmit something to the same people.

Although there are submission-tracking programs available, they're unnecessary. Open a simple word processing file, type your project's title centered at the top, and then create a line underneath it with the following information:

Name of Project

Item Sent	Date Sent	Where Sent	Date of Response	Type of Response

Item Sent refers to your request for guidelines, your query letter, your proposal, your follow-up note, or your completed manuscript. It's a simple enough job to fill in the information under each heading.

Can You Resubmit Once Your Idea Has Been Turned Down?

Yes—to publishers. Sometimes an idea arrives on an editor's desk at the wrong time. The editor just signed a similar book (which later falls through). The editor has been told to limit the number of new acquisitions. There's a rumor that a particular house imprint might fold. The editor might be getting ready to go on vacation. The editor might be moving up the ladder—or out the door. If your research shows you that your book would fit nicely with a particular house, don't be shy about trying later—but make it much later. Wait at least a year before querying again. This gives attitudes a chance to change. Tie a current event to the material to highlight the timeliness of the project.

With agents, there's not much reason to submit your query to the same one twice. Most have pretty good memories and they'll remember your previous query. If they didn't like your idea then, they probably won't like it now.

Turnoffs

All new writers make mistakes when learning how to write and market their material. This is understood and, in most cases, forgiven. However, some mistakes can show a lack of professionalism and an attitude that agents and editors won't want to work with.

Here several agents reveal what in a writer's approach can be a turnoff.

Simon Lipskar

"A couple of things come to mind. One is the author who appears more interested in grandiose schemes for marketing and promotion than he is in producing a quality proposal or book. Another is the author who tackles a topic he has neither the qualifications nor platform to address.

"Something else that drives me crazy is at the end of the letter saying, 'I am a real writer, a real professional writer. I plan on writing books for a long time. In fact, I already have a sequel to the book I'm working on.'"

Jessica Faust

"Too cute. I don't read cover letters and manuscripts because they are cute and friendly; I read them because your description of your book and your credentials captured my attention. I don't want to hear that all of your friends loved the book, I don't need chocolates or flowers, and I don't need to know that your dream is to get this book published."

Do not put the copyright symbol anywhere on your material: not in your letters, your proposal, or your finished manuscript. Your work is automatically covered by copyright laws; using the symbol brands you an amateur. It also shows a degree of mistrust that can put off editors and agents.

Ellen Geiger

"Overreaching. Proposing something they're not really qualified to write about. Not doing their homework regarding what else is on the market in their area. Not developing a marketing strategy early on. Claiming that *everyone* will be interested in their book—which shows both grandiosity and naïveté. Bad writing. Hubris. And last but not least, badgering the agent, which is a total turnoff."

David Duperre

"The biggest mistakes most new nonfiction writers make is not knowing their subject and not fleshing out the manuscript. Ego is great but has a time and place. Telling a publisher how great a writer you are won't get his attention as much as showing him how great a writer you are! In other words, put your story where your mouth is!"

Dorian Karchmar

"Turnoffs are boasting, arrogance, impatience, lack of professionalism, and ignorance of the industry and their market/genre.

"Mistakes are working for years writing a manuscript (rather than proposal) for which they are not qualified or for which they have no platform to promote. If you're a linguist, don't write a book about parenting—unless it's better-parenting-through-the-use-of-language.

"Also, approaching agents too early in the process—before they have started working on the proposal; before they have developed the necessary credentials/expertise; before they have developed their writing craft as fully as they need to; before they have fully conceptualized and hammered out what their project is and who will buy it."

Sample Query Letters and Proposals

"The task of an American writer is not to describe the misgivings of a woman taken in adultery as she looks out of a window at the rain, but to describe four hundred people under the lights reaching for a foul ball. This is ceremony."

—John Cheever

IN THIS CHAPTER you will find examples of three successful query letters and proposals. (This means they each landed an agent or a book contract.) For privacy reasons, letterhead and other address information have been left out. Because of length and copyright constraints, the sample chapters that usually accompany a book proposal are not included here.

Note that one-page query letters are single-spaced and book proposals are double-spaced. Both should be on 8½ × 11 paper. (You will see that the query letters in these proposals run longer than one page each. This is due to the reduced trim size of this book. These query letters would fit on one page if they were printed on 8½ × 11 paper.)

Not all of the query letters included here are 100 percent perfect. Some make mistakes this book warns against. The advice offered throughout this book aims for a general account of the publishing process and the kinds of things that appeal to a wide range of agents and publishers. But keep in mind that all agents and editors have their own unique likes and dislikes, and something that will appeal to one won't necessarily appeal to another working within the same category. They will make allowances, though. In the end, if your book idea is sound and your credentials convince them you should be the author of the book, your query and proposal will find an ear.

Query Letter and Proposal Sample #1

Gail Rubin landed her new agent for *A Girl's Pocket Guide to Trouser Trout* after meeting her at a conference and sending her this proposal. The query letter, outline, and first two chapters won first prize for nonfiction in the 2000 SouthWest Writers annual writing contest. The book is just beginning to make the rounds of publishers. Says the author, "I had actually written the book before the proposal; not the way to do it, I now know. Since this is a work of creative nonfiction, I didn't know exactly what the book would contain until I had written it."

This query letter's opening paragraph contains the hook, and the third paragraph contains the handle. The query letter is so well written and contains such intriguing information that it's not surprising the author is now agented. Expect to see this book on bookstore shelves soon.

Dear _____:

If men were fish and women the anglers who caught them, what kind of men would you know? Colorful, athletic rainbow trout or manic flying fish? Talkative sea trout or egotistical blowfish? "Nice guy" lake trout or passive urchins? Perhaps they've got the stamina of a steelhead or the characteristics of a cutthroat?

A Girl's Pocket Guide to Trouser Trout can help a woman define her own angling style in the search for that special trophy trout, with information on other fish in the sea to avoid; quality streams to fish (good places to meet good men); leader lines (what to say first); and natural, artificial, and exotic lures. What to do when the fishing hole runs dry, prospects for angling in the later years, trouser trout tips, and tall tales of trout landed or lost round out the manuscript.

Imagine the nineties relationship bestseller *The Rules* or Cynthia Heimel's 1986 bestseller *Sex Tips for Girls* crossed with Izaak Walton's seventeenth-century fishing classic *The Compleat Angler* and you have some idea of my approach. *A Girl's Pocket Guide to Trouser Trout* takes the dating concept of "fishing for a good catch" literally and ties the search for Mr. Right to angling activities.

With more than twenty-five years of trouser trout
angling experience, I've dated my share of blowfish, crabs, and urchins, as well as some really
swell trouser trout. Once married and divorced, I
cast for a keeper for twelve years and have
finally landed my trophy trout.

Would you be interested in seeing a proposal and
the first three chapters of *A Girl's Pocket Guide
to Trouser Trout*?

Sincerely,
Gail Rubin
Gail Rubin

Book Proposal:

A Girl's Pocket Guide to Trouser Trout:

Reflections on Dating and

Fly-Fishing

by Gail Rubin

Proposal Table of Contents

Overview   Page 1

Format   Page 3

The Market   Page 5

The Competition   Page 7

Author Biography   Page 9

Author Promotion   Page 10

Table of Contents   Page 12

Chapter Summaries   Page 14

OVERVIEW

What if men were fish and women the anglers who catch them? The savvy angler would have *A Girl's Pocket Guide to Trouser Trout* at her bedside to teach her how to find and catch the keepers. Imagine the nineties relationship bestseller *The Rules* or Cynthia Heimel's 1986 bestseller *Sex Tips for Girls* crossed with Izaak Walton's seventeenth-century fishing classic, *The Compleat Angler*, and you have some idea of my approach. *A Girl's Pocket Guide to Trouser Trout* takes the dating concept of "fishing for a good catch" literally and ties the search for Mr. Right to angling activities.

Trout are the kind of fellows women want to meet—colorful, athletic rainbows or opinionated browns, family-minded brookies or spiritual salmon. Perhaps an angler's trophy trout has the characteristics of a cutthroat or the stamina of a steelhead. But not all men are trout. The other fish in the sea make women's lives miserable—the crabs, clams, bottom feeders, blowfish, trash fish—you get the idea.

A Girl's Pocket Guide to Trouser Trout can help a woman define her own angling style in the search for that special trophy trout, with information on quality streams to fish (good places to meet good men); leader lines (what to say first); and natural, artificial, and exotic lures (how to get their attention). What to do when the fishing hole runs dry, prospects for angling in the later years, and tall tales of trout landed or lost round out the manuscript.

A Girl's Pocket Guide to Trouser Trout shines a light into the sometimes-murky waters of modern dating and relationships.

In September 2000, the book was awarded first place in the nonfiction book category of the highly regarded writing contest held by SouthWest Writers (formerly Southwest Writers Workshop).

Rubin/Proposal for *A Girl's Pocket Guide to . . .*   3

Nonfiction book contest judge Wendy Knerr, editor
of the Writer's Digest Book Club, said in her
critique, "You've done your research, and it
shows. . . . Your metaphors are consistent and
don't get tired, which is to be commended.
Congratulations!"

FORMAT

The manuscript runs about 40,000 words with an
introduction and ten chapters. Each chapter contains quotes from fishing books and angling publications that provide insights into the nature
of relationships, even though the quotes were
written about fishing. Short fiction scenarios in
each chapter that follow the adventures of
trouser trout anglers Amy, Margo, and Helen help
illustrate the book's many parallels between
fishing and relationships. Examples of these comparisons include:

Rubin/Proposal for *A Girl's Pocket Guide to . . .*   4

- Descriptions for types of trout and other fish in the sea, comparing the characteristics of water-based creatures to land-based menfolk
- Quality streams to fish for trouser trout
- Natural, artificial, and exotic lures to attract trouser trout, with tips on "presentation" and "matching the hatch"
- A quiz for women to determine if a man is a trout or another fish in the sea
- A comparison of wading and dating techniques
- Reasons trout and trouser trout don't rise to the lure
- Q&A with trouser trout angling expert Dr. Sandy Bottoms

The manuscript's back matter includes a glossary of definitions for fishing and trouser trout angling, running the alphabetical gamut from

Rubin/Proposal for *A Girl's Pocket Guide to . . .*   5

attractor to *trolling*, a bibliography, and a recommended reading list on fishing and relationships.

THE MARKET

A Girl's Pocket Guide to Trouser Trout will
appeal to two markets. The primary market is
adult women—a huge market by itself—from
college-age *nymphs* to older, experienced
spinners. In addition to single women, almost
half of baby boomers, about 25 million American
men and women, have been married and divorced,
and many are casting about for their next catch.

This is also the kind of book married women
would want to give to their single girlfriends
for support and comic relief.

The secondary market is trout fishing
enthusiasts, both male and female. Fly-fishing
as a recreation has garnered thousands of
novices in the past few years, and interest in
the sport continues to grow.

Rubin/Proposal for *A Girl's Pocket Guide to* . . .   6

A survey in *Fly Fisherman* magazine reported:

- Fly fishers reside in approximately 13 million U.S. households, equating to 13.5 percent of the population.
- The most enthusiastic hardcore group of fly fishers comprises at least 600,000 females and 5.7 million males.
- There was a 30 percent growth in the sport between 1993 and 1995, mostly women in pre- and post-child-raising phases of their lives.
- The number of women who have taken up fly-fishing has accelerated during the 1990s.
- News coverage of women fly-fishing has increased correspondingly.

If the book appealed only to fly fishers, it would still have an impressive audience.

Rubin/Proposal for *A Girl's Pocket Guide to . . .*   7

Together with the primary market, the number of potential purchasers is significant.

THE COMPETITION

In the 1990s, hundreds of book titles were published on dating and relationships. Almost as many books were published on fly-fishing during that time. While recent relationship books take different approaches, some serious and some humorous, no nonfiction books on the market directly draw parallels from dating to the growing sport of fly-fishing.

A search of Amazon.com with the key word "dating" yielded 1,629 entries. These titles ranged from hundreds of nonfiction dating and relationship books to scholarly dissertations on isotope dating techniques to Sweet Valley High novels for teens. The topic is very popular.

The 1997 nonfiction book *Catch & Release: The Insider's Guide to Alaska Men* may be the most similar title on the market. The 1998 bestselling novel *Animal Husbandry*, which is being made into a film, draws parallels between animal behavior and human male-female relationships. The 1999 bestselling fiction story collection *The Girl's Guide to Hunting and Fishing* demonstrates the appeal of humorous stories with a fishing and relationship motif.

A Girl's Pocket Guide to Trouser Trout touches on the topics explored in top sellers such as *Get a Life, Then Get a Man: A Single Woman's Guide*; *Date Like a Man to Get the Man You Want and Have Fun Doing It*; *Dating for Dummies*; *The Complete Idiot's Guide to Dating*; . . . to *Handling a Breakup*; and . . . *Online Dating and Relating*.

A Girl's Pocket Guide to Trouser Trout will be the first how-to book for women that brings

together the wisdom, warmth, and humor in
fishing lore to the topic of relationships.

AUTHOR BIOGRAPHY

Author Gail Rubin has more than twenty-five
years of trouser trout angling experience. Once
married and divorced, she has dated her share
of blowfish, crabs, and urchins, as well as
some really swell trouser trout. After twelve
years of casting for a keeper, she landed her
trophy trout and was married in December 2000.

A public relations professional with more
than fifteen years of national promotional
experience, Gail Rubin knows how to promote her
own book. Clients she has worked with include
The Discovery Channel; The History Channel; Home
Box Office; National Geographic Television;
Lockheed Martin (for the John Glenn/Space Shuttle
Discovery launch and annual Space Day celebra-
tions); major public television stations; and

Rubin/Proposal for *A Girl's Pocket Guide to* . . .   10

authors such as Tom Peters, famous for his many business management bestsellers, and children's author and musician Barry Louis Polisar. She holds a B.A. in communications and English from the University of Maryland, College Park.

She was the 1999 vice president of SouthWest Writers (formerly Southwest Writers Workshop), a 1,000+ member teaching organization for writers. She has published bylined articles in a wide range of publications, including *The Albuquerque Journal*, *Catholic Digest*, the Jewish Telegraphic Agency newswire, and *Momentum* magazine. She was also a television producer with C-SPAN for five years, booking guests on the network's national call-in program and writing articles about Congressional activities.

AUTHOR PROMOTION

As an experienced public relations professional, the author is highly qualified to undertake a comprehensive media program to garner exposure for *A Girl's Pocket Guide to Trouser Trout*, including:

- Creating a comprehensive press kit for the book—news release, tip sheets, selected quotes, photograph of author, and press clips.
- Pitching news stories about the book and offering author interviews to print and broadcast media.
- Speaking before specialized audiences, such as singles events, comedy clubs, and fishing organizations.

A Girl's Pocket Guide to Trouser Trout can be successfully promoted through multiple channels:

- Women's and men's magazines
- Fishing publications
- Evening and daytime TV talk shows
- Radio talk shows, especially with "shock jocks" and fishing programs

Rubin/Proposal for *A Girl's Pocket Guide to . . .*   12

- Book reviews and style section profiles in
  newspapers
- Teaching noncredit special interest classes

In addition to traditional book signing
appearances in stores, sportsmen's shows—events
to which many men bring their wives—are good
candidates for book sales and signing events.
Author talks at fishing organization meetings
and outdoor outfitter stores and singles
events, tied in with local media interviews,
are other possible promotional venues.

TABLE OF CONTENTS

Introduction: Trouser Trout Fishing in America

Chapter 1: Your Personal Angling Style

Chapter 2: Types o' Trout

Chapter 3: The Compleat Angler: Natural, Artifi-
            cial, and Exotic Lures

Chapter 4: Where the Lunkers Lurk: Trouser Trout
            Habitat

Rubin/Proposal for *A Girl's Pocket Guide to . . .*   13

Chapter 5: Stalking the Wily Trout: Angling Tactics

Chapter 6: A River Runs Through It: Trouser

Trout Tips

Chapter 7: Whatcha Gonna Do When the Hole Runs

Dry?: Angling Advice

Chapter 8: It Was This Big!: Adventures in

Trouser Trout Angling

Chapter 9: On Golden Pond: Angling As Time Goes By

Chapter 10: Happy Fishing: May Your Lunker Line

Always Be Full

CHAPTER SUMMARIES

Introduction: Trouser Trout Fishing in America

The introduction lays out the book's concept,
that good men are trouser trout and women are the
anglers who catch them. Dame Juliana Berners, a
nun and noblewoman, wrote *The Treatise on Fishing
with an Angle*, the first English text on fly-
fishing, in about 1425. Her keen observations
about human nature and fishing, along with quotes
from numerous other angling authors, help illumi-
nate the nature of modern dating and relationships as we dive into the wide wet world of
trouser trout angling.

Chapter 1: Your Personal Angling Style

Are you the kind of gal who knows what she wants
and sets out to get it, or would you rather wait
for someone to come along and change your life
for you? Are you content to fish alone and get an
occasional strike, or do you feel incomplete if

you don't have a trout on the line? Many motivations and paths influence the angler's approach to the trouser trout tango. This chapter details angling behavior for different types of women and reasons why women go trouser trout angling.

Chapter 2: Types o' Trout

This chapter provides comparisons of types of trout and kinds of men, and how to recognize them in the field. Among the twelve species described are Rainbow (athletic, colorful characters), Brown (transplanted or Euro-trout), Cutthroat (circumcised trout), Golden (rich trout), and Dolly Varden (cross-dressers), plus relatives such as Salmon (spiritual trout), Whitefish (intellectuals), and Grayling (elder trout). Quotes from fishing books provide apt descriptions that apply to both men and fish. The trout represents the nobler aspects of a man, while negative characteristics are embodied by the

Rubin/Proposal for *A Girl's Pocket Guide to . . .*　　16

other fish in the sea. These include bottom feeders (abusers), blowfish (egotistical farts),
urchins (helpless invertebrates), octopi (smoth-
ering invertebrates), and carp (constant com-
plainers). A multiple-choice quiz helps readers
determine where a man lands in the spectrum of
trout versus other fish in the sea. Behavioral
similarities between trout and men in their home
habitat are also included.

Chapter 3: The Compleat Angler: Natural,
Artificial, and Exotic Lures

Fur, feathers, silk, and leather, the range of
lures is wide, deep, and seasonal. Any prepared
angler will have lures—trouser trout flies, if
you will--in her tackle box. This chapter covers
matching the hatch (meeting expectations and pro-
jecting a particular image to hook the type of
trout you want) with details on attractors (colorful lures and knowing what looks best on you),

live bait (dogs and exotic pets), hardware (jewelry and accessories), hairstyles, fancy footwear, lingerie lures, and synthetic lures (implants and plastic surgery), as well as culinary and conversational lures.

Chapter 4: Where the Lunkers Lurk: Trouser Trout Habitat

This chapter covers where to find trout and avoid those other fish in the sea: quality streams (the good places to meet men, some of which may have been recommended by your mother), stock and pull streams (the obvious places, with less-than-stellar trouser trout), personal ads, and online angling for cybertrout.

Chapter 5: Stalking the Wily Trout: Angling Tactics

As any good fisherman knows, you don't stomp up to a stream and thrash about. That scares off the trout. Proper presentation is everything. This chapter focuses on techniques: using a specific lure versus casting a wide net, finding a trout that's already looking, casting approaches, fishing etiquette, and no-nos.

Chapter 6: A River Runs Through It:

Trouser Trout Tips

This chapter covers relationship specifics for trouser trout anglers, from initiating a strike to landing one's catch. Topics include setting the hook and reeling him in, recognizing when to toss one back, legal limits on catches, trouser trout lore, the importance of condoms in this age of polluted water, dealing with dead trout, Lorena Bobbitt and Bob's two-bit taxidermy advice, and dating tips for clueless trout.

Chapter 7: Whatcha Gonna Do When the Hole Runs Dry?: Angling Advice

When a trouser trout angler comes up empty-handed, there's usually a plausible explanation. This chapter includes nine reasons a fish may not rise to the lure, from a 1907 issue of *Field & Stream*, with trouser trout interpretations. My alter ego, noted trouser trout expert Dr. Sandy Bottoms (a woman who knows, in sordid detail, what puts the "ick" in ichthyology), answers questions regarding trout and other fish in the sea. Her no-nonsense advice gladdens the hearts of frustrated trouser trout anglers faced with poor fishing conditions.

Chapter 8: It Was This Big!: Adventures in Trouser Trout Angling

What trouser trout angler doesn't have at least one big fish story, whether it slipped off into

Rubin/Proposal for *A Girl's Pocket Guide to . . .*   20

the deep or came home as a keeper to be mounted

for posterity? Three trouser trout anglers tell

their tallest tales and discuss the secrets to

their success. From international romance to the

man that got away, their stories showcase high

adventure in trouser trout angling.

Chapter 9: On Golden Pond: Angling

As Time Goes By

Trouser trout fishing is not just for the young.

As our baby boom population ages, we are seeing

greater numbers of older anglers casting their

lines into the dating pool. This chapter touches

on the phenomenon of selective feeding (we become

pickier as we get older), differences in approach

taken by nymph anglers versus spinners (young

women versus older, experienced women), and

trouser trout angling past the midlife crisis.

Chapter 10: Happy Fishing: May Your Lunker Line Always Be Full

In life and love, as in fishing, there are good days and bad days. We treasure the moments of serenity and electric connection, and minimize the discomforts and hassles of the angling experience. Why else would we keep coming back to do it again and again? This chapter presents a thoughtful, upbeat conclusion on the art of trouser trout angling.

Glossary: Trouser trout interpretations of common angling terms.

Bibliography/Recommended Reading List: Works consulted and recommended reading on life, love, and trout fishing.

Query Letter and Proposal Sample #2

As described in Chapter 3, agent Dorian Karchmar helped author Roger Goldberg refocus his proposal to narrow the audience and find a catchier title. The query letter here refers to the title the author originally suggested and also contains a quote from the proposal that was later revised.

The query letter is addressed to the agency director. Although more effusive than necessary, the first paragraph reflects that a prior contact was made and that the proposal was solicited. The final paragraphs show the author knows his audience.

Ever Since I Had My Baby is tentatively scheduled for a fall 2002 release from Crown Books.

Dear _____:

As an overworked surgeon and avid writer, I thank
you in advance for devoting a few moments of your
busy schedule to consider my proposal. I am confident that in sharing with you a portion of my
manuscript, I am wasting neither your time nor
your energy, which I know to be precious commodi-
ties. Based on my discussion with Dorian last
week and her description of Lowenstein Associates
and your professional interests, it is clear that
I could not have chosen a more suitable agency to
review my work.

My specialty, pelvic reconstructive surgery and
urogynecology, is the burgeoning area of women's
health care devoted to the treatment and research
of pelvic floor disorders—that is, the physical
repercussions of childbirth. I am in the process
of completing a manuscript, the first of its
kind, written for millions of women affected by
incontinence and prolapse, among other conditions, which largely stem from labor and delivery. They are, overall, among the most common
conditions suffered within the female population,
yet among the least discussed. In caring for
patients with prolapse and incontinence in my
daily practice, I am constantly asked the questions, "Why wasn't I told about this before I had
my baby?" and "Where can I read more about this?"
Surprisingly, to date, no such book has been

written. Yet, as the enclosed About the Book section (of the proposal) reads:

> At this moment on the evolutionary clock of women's health care, this major issue is emerging into the medical spotlight. . . . If these problems sound esoteric, rest assured that they are not. If you haven't heard a great deal about them, stay tuned—you will. The issue of obstetrical injury, just beginning to form ripples in the medical waters, is a whale about to surface.

The time is ripe for *What to Expect After You've Expected—A Women's Guide to Urogynecology and the Neglected Epidemic of Childbirth Injury*. *What to Expect* is a woman's guide to these neglected areas of postreproductive health, the first comprehensive, practical guide to the prevention and treatment of problems related to childbirth. It is a call for more candid discussion, investigation, and prevention in a medical field that, until today, has been characterized by injury, disability, and repair. It provides the first available self-help resource for countless postreproductive women and for younger women raised in an era of preventive health, looking ahead to childbearing.

As a physician, researcher, and writer, I am confident in my ability to produce a highly provocative, engaging, and genuinely significant work with mass appeal. As a more than casual daily

observer of the medical dilemmas faced by this
largest postreproductive female population in
history, I am absolutely confident of this book's
market. I have enclosed an expanded outline with
sample chapters, along with my curriculum vitae.
I look forward to your feedback and hope I'll
have the opportunity to work with you in producing a final book of outstanding quality and great
commercial success.

Respectfully yours,
Roger P. Goldberg
Roger P. Goldberg, M.D., M.P.H.

Book Proposal:

Ever Since I Had My Baby:

A Woman's Complete Guide to Treating and

Preventing the Most Common Physical

Aftereffects of Childbirth

by Roger P. Goldberg, M.D., M.P.H.

Division of Reconstructive Pelvic Surgery

and Urogynecology

Department of Obstetrics and Gynecology

Northwestern University Medical School

Proposal Table of Contents*

About the Author

About the Book and Market

Publishing Details

The Competition

Condensed Table of Contents

Preface

Chapter Excerpts

Author's Curriculum Vitae

*The preface, chapter excerpts, and author's curriculum vitae have been omitted from this sample.

ABOUT THE AUTHOR

Dr. Roger Goldberg practices reconstructive
pelvic surgery and urogynecology at the Evanston
Continence Center of Northwestern University Medical School. He received his residency training
at Harvard University's Beth Israel Hospital and
a master's of public health degree in reproductive epidemiology from Johns Hopkins School of
Public Health and Hygiene. As an associate at one
of the nation's most active centers for female
continence and gynecological surgery, he actively
publishes articles and book chapters and regularly presents original research at international
venues, including Rome, Finland, and Athens. His
research interests include the surgical treatment
of genital prolapse and incontinence and the
obstetrical risk factors leading to these disorders in later life. Since earning his undergradu-
ate degree in English literature from Cornell
University, he has remained an avid writer. He

and his wife, Elena, live in Chicago with their
mutt, Chester.

ABOUT THE BOOK AND MARKET: "WHERE CAN I READ MORE ABOUT THIS?"

Across cultures, continents, and generations, the
birth of a newborn is a human moment that ele-
vates us and provides our single clearest glimpse
into the divine. What other experience throughout
the human life cycle so universally suspends our
cynicism and rekindles the possibilities of wonder and miracle? Yet, on a less ethereal plane,
labor and delivery also represent a monumental
physical strain. Whereas most of our physical
alterations accumulate gradually across the years
and decades of our adulthood, during childbirth
we witness dramatic changes occurring right
before our eyes.

Not without consequence. Along the winding
road between childbirth and menopause, scores of

women find themselves affected by problems
attributable to the labor room, attesting to the
extraordinary physical demands of pregnancy,
labor, and delivery. Some of these changes
involving the lower half of the body are subtle,
and others are severe. Some "postreproductive"
changes are immediately apparent, affecting the
quality of a woman's most vigorous years; for
others, it may only be decades later that they
first begin to notice symptoms, which can, in
fact, be traced back to the delivery suite.
Whether these physical transitions are subtle or
severe, immediate or delayed, they are rarely
expected and even more seldom understood. And
over just the past several years, we've come to
understand that these problems are far more common, and certainly more significant, than we'd
ever acknowledged. At this moment, women in their
thirties, forties, fifties, and beyond are emerging from the shadows in great numbers, seeking

Goldberg/Proposal for *Ever Since I Had My Baby* 4

solutions for problems of the lower body, which, in many cases, they had overlooked since the day they left the maternity ward:

• **Urinary Incontinence** (loss of control over urine). One of every three women will suffer significant loss of bladder control, and up to 65 percent will notice this problem for the first time either during or after childbirth. Millions each year choose surgery for this debilitating symptom, and millions seek nonsurgical treatments; countless others silently endure their loss of control without ever seeking help.

• **Prolapse** ("dropping" of the uterus, bladder, and vagina). Remarkably, up to 11 percent of the entire female population will undergo *major surgery* for prolapse—a number roughly equal to the lifetime risk of breast cancer. And for each woman choosing surgery, many others seek "conser-

Goldberg/Proposal for *Ever Since I Had My Baby*   5

vative" therapy for these problems, which result
from weakening of the pelvic floor, usually a
result of pregnancy and delivery.

• **Anal Incontinence** (loss of control over
feces, or gas). Neglected by physicians, who fail
to address these issues with patients, and
endured by patients feeling too embarrassed to
mention it, the problem remains underdiagnosed—
and childbirth injury is considered the most common predisposing factor in women.

• **Loss of Sexual Satisfaction.** Entering
postreproductive life, a surprising number of
women view their diminished sexual satisfaction
and pleasure as an inevitable aspect of a postreproductive body—unaware of not only the physical
changes accounting for their problem but also of
the preventive strategies and many effective

treatments that exist, both before and after childbirth.

• **Other Changes "Down There."** Finally, countless women notice something else has changed after childbirth around the pelvis, bladder, vagina, or bowel. For some, it was an episiotomy that never felt fully healed, pelvic pain, or an overactive bladder starting to wake them from sleep throughout the night. For others, it was a symptom they'd never associated with the physical stress of pregnancy, labor, and delivery—such as constipation, vaginal dryness, or recurrent vaginal or bladder infections. But each of these and others, in fact, might have been caused or exacerbated by childbirth—and understanding this provides the basis for most effectively preventing, ameliorating, and curing them.

The First Postobstetrical Guidebook for Women

At nearly every stage throughout their reproductive lives, women have a "guide" available on the bookshelf to help navigate the road they feel twisting in ways unexpected. This particular guide to the most commonplace aftereffects of labor and delivery has not yet been written, and its potential audience is tremendous. For the younger woman contemplating pregnancy, one in the midst of her childbearing years, or one looking back upon childbirth to realize that it marked the beginning of new problems that made life a bit less carefree—*this book is for her*.

For the baby boomer convinced that "those problems" her mother dealt with are still inevitable milestones of perimenopause—*read on*. There are countless ways to treat, reverse, and sometimes even prevent these conditions, beginning right in her own home. Promoting health in the most intimate areas of her body, maintaining control over

Goldberg/Proposal for *Ever Since I Had My Baby*   8

her most basic bodily functions, and preserving
her sense of youth and sexuality—these goals
deserve a place in her health planning. After all,
as women of her generation begin facing a postreproductive lifetime spanning decades, rather than
only years, there will be an ever-increasing need
to effectively treat whatever physical changes may
have occurred in the labor room.

At this moment in the evolution of women's
health care, the physical repercussions of childbirth have been thrust directly into the medical
spotlight; women are, at last, openly discussing
these "dirty little secrets," which have for so
long been ignored. Incontinence, prolapse, and
other postreproductive disorders have finally
been recognized as a major public health burden
accounting for billions of health care dollars
and immeasurable humiliation, loss of self-
esteem, and social withdrawal. In fact, the sub-
specialty of urogynecology coalesced, over the

past few years, to meet the sharply increased
demand for the effective treatment of incontinence, prolapse, and other complications of
pelvic floor injury. And just this year, the
National Institutes of Health (NIH) devoted $10
million to the study of pelvic floor disorders,
making it arguably our top national priority in
women's health. Though only yesterday they were
little spoken of, the female conditions triggered
by childbirth account today for one of the most
rapidly growing medical and surgical subspecialties, and one of the "hottest" items on the
national women's health agenda. If these problems
sound esoteric, rest assured that they are not.
If you haven't heard a great deal about them,
stay tuned—you will. The issue of obstetrical
injury, just beginning to form ripples in the
medical waters, is a whale about to surface.

As a surgeon, clinician, and researcher in
this field, I am constantly asked the questions

"Why wasn't I told about this before I had my baby?" and "Where can I read more about this?" "What," these women wonder, "can be done to beat the odds, and avoid these problems that I've seen my mother and her friends deal with?" Surprisingly, to date, no such book has been written, despite a current wave of medical research that is rapidly expanding our understanding of obstetrical injury and its aftermath. As a result, affected women and concerned family members have had no means to educate themselves. After all, according to national data, only one in five women with these symptoms will overcome the stigma and see a specialist; among those remaining, there exists a tremendous demand for explanations, reassurance, and self-help strategies that can be found outside the doctor's office. Invariably, women who have found help are amazed to discover the world of treatments available for ameliorating, preventing, or at least coping with

the major changes that can follow childbirth. And
they feel relieved and grateful to have these
problems finally acknowledged. *There is no book
yet on the shelf that connects the disconnect
between childbirth and pelvic floor injury—
indeed, between obstetrics and gynecology.* Given
the scope and prevalence of pelvic floor dysfunction among this huge cohort and the lack of self-
help information accessible to them, the market
is ripe for *Ever Since I Had My Baby.*

The Audience

The book is geared toward two major demographic
groups: young women of childbearing age and baby
boomers forty and up. For younger women in their
childbearing years, the book offers information
on obstetrical injury, a topic that is *seldom, if
ever,* discussed during prenatal care or included
in pregnancy guides. Self-help books, such as
What to Expect While You're Expecting, have

proven the tremendous literary market potential within this demographic sector. Women of reproductive age will be fascinated to learn what can be done *before, during, and after* delivery to most fully maintain their gynecological, urological, and even sexual health. In fact, according to a recently published survey of reproductive-age women, an overwhelming 83 percent reported they would like to be provided with information regarding the postnatal risk of prolapse and incontinence. Surprisingly, no source for this information yet exists on the bookshelves. For a generation of young women increasingly determined to prevent disease and maintain vigor rather than quietly accept the physical marks of aging, the notion of "preventive obstetrical care" is long overdue. This book may represent its seedling.

For female boomers, the book fills a void left virtually untouched by existing menopause guides. Capturing this medical moment at which childbirth and its aftereffects have been united in the doctor's office and operating room, *Ever Since I Had My Baby* will be the first book to thrust this perspective into the mainstream spotlight. Over the next decade, nearly 80 million female baby boomers will reach menopause, representing the largest postreproductive female population ever to exist. As the fastest expanding segment of our population, they are expected to account for nearly a quarter of the United States by 2040. Female boomers have proven themselves, at every life stage, to be highly insightful, medically curious, politically organized—and eager to read, when it concerns breakthrough issues affecting their health. Theirs is the generation that embraced *Our Bodies, Ourselves* during the sexual revolution, and more recently, Dr. Susan Love's bestsellers on breast disease and hormone replacement. *Ever Since I Had My Baby* follows in this tradition, covering uncharted literary territory. It is the

first comprehensive self-help resource for scores
of women who experienced physical changes after
childbirth—a practical guide providing long-
overdue explanations and therapeutic alternatives
found not only in the operating room and doctor's
office but also at home.

Content and Style

A blend of anecdote-rich text and illustrations
will cover an introduction to pelvic anatomy, the
progress of "normal" labor, and the physical
changes that most commonly occur during childbirth. Readers find concise descriptions and
illustrations clarifying what has happened, when
this happened, and how this happened. The very
challenging topics of pelvic anatomy and the
physical changes seen after delivery are presented in an easily understandable way. Strategies are geared toward both the prevention of
pelvic floor injuries and the treatment of those

that have already occurred. The reader is handed
a toolbox full of self-help strategies ranging
from simple dietary changes to exercises, healthy
habits, home remedies, and alternative therapy.
Office visits and outpatient testing are
explained, followed by an array of noninvasive
treatments ranging from pelvic floor exercises
and biofeedback to electrical and magnetic pelvic
floor rehabilitation, vaginal devices, and colla-
gen injections. The ever-expanding options for
surgical treatment are then clearly presented,
with an emphasis on "what to expect" and "how
you'll feel." The medical content within *Ever
Since I Had My Baby* is comprehensive, yet totally
inviting and reassuring in its presentation,
filled with accessible anecdotes appropriate for
every reading demographic, with the intention of
conveying to the reader "No, you're not alone,"
and "Yes, there are solutions."

Finally, the book will touch on the political and economic forces that have entered the delivery room in recent years—that is, the "invisible obstetricians" powerfully influencing patients, physicians, and our choices surrounding these postobstetrical problems. Why, the question is asked, haven't I heard about these issues until now . . . and why have they been so casually regarded as "normal"? Readers may be surprised to learn the degree to which economic, societal, and political factors, from both the right and the left, can often influence obstetrical trends more powerfully than the impact of hard scientific evidence. And they will be even more surprised to understand the lasting effect of these obstetrical trends on their own bodies. Perhaps only through childbirth do politics, ethics, and economics intersect with biology and health in such eternally compelling ways.

The book's content lends itself to future editions, revised to meet the needs and concerns of the "boomlet" generation following at the heels of the baby boomers. After all, as this book is completed during the next twelve months alone, 4.7 million of these active and affluent Americans will turn forty, representing a birthday celebration every 6.5 seconds. Before long, this female population, the largest in its age category ever to exist, will arrive at the front gates of their golden years facing the same set of physical problems, undoubtedly eager to discuss their own unique concerns, and the latest alternatives for prevention, preparation, and treatment. The potential commercial longevity for this seminal postobstetrical guide is boundless, considering the fundamental medical content at its core, involving millions of women and billions of dollars.

Goldberg/Proposal for *Ever Since I Had My Baby*   18

For countless women touched today by the widespread conditions associated with postobstetrical changes and hungry to restore their sense of health, dignity, and sexuality, here is the first book written for them. For women looking ahead to childbirth, here is a fresh and compelling new voice on the bookshelves, focused specifically on their bodies and future function. With a readership spanning from expectant mothers, through childbirth, postpartum, and menopause, *Ever Since I Had My Baby* is an essential addition to the literature of women's health.

PUBLISHING DETAILS

Ever Since I Had My Baby will be approximately three hundred pages long, with one to three illustrations per chapter. Each chapter is prefaced with a quote, most from actual patients. Numerous text boxes containing interesting facts and "take home" messages are interspersed within

various chapters. The glossary provides a quick
reference for relevant medical terminology, and
the appendix references various support groups
and online resources. The book will be fully completed no more than a year following the request
for manuscript.

THE COMPETITION

As a surgeon and researcher operating on the
"front lines" of this rapidly growing medical
field, I can confidently conclude that there are
no similar books on the market. Within the scientific press, recent years have seen the publication of several textbooks geared toward health
care providers, reflecting the rapidly expanding
market demand in this area of clinical medicine.
For instance, *Female Pelvic Floor Disorders* by J.
Thomas Benson (W. W. Norton) and *The Female
Pelvic Floor: Disorders of Function and Support*
by Linda Brubaker (F. A. Davis) were both

authored by well-respected urogynecologists who recognized the rapidly rising wave of interest among doctors and nurses in these postreproductive problems. But neither of these books addressed the largest potential audience of interested readers: *the patient.*

Few mainstream books, in fact, from pregnancy manuals to menopause guides, have included more than passing references to the physical repercussions of pregnancy on the pelvis, bladder, and vagina. And none of them has bridged the disconnect between these physical changes and the postreproductive problems—including incontinence, prolapse, and sexual dysfunction—suddenly receiving so much attention at this moment in women's health. *The Girlfriends' Guide to Pregnancy: Or Everything Your Doctor Won't Tell You* by Vicki Iovine (Pocket Books Childcare) allocates only two short paragraphs of the book's last page to these topics. *What to Expect While*

You're Expecting (Workman Publishing Company) makes only a quick half-page reference to the issue of "being stretched by childbirth" and the role of Kegel exercises during pregnancy.

Within the "new motherhood" literary genre, Sheila Kitzinger's *The Year After Childbirth* (Fireside, Simon & Schuster) devotes a sixteen-page chapter to recovery of the pelvic floor after childbirth. However, its scope is limited to symptoms during the first year after delivery and fails to address the most central question: What happens to the woman who *doesn't* fully recover? Finally, even commercially successful perimenopause guides contain a surprising lack of information on these cutting-edge topics. For instance, in Judith Reichman's *I'm Too Young to Get Old* (Times Books), the "changes after forty" center around hormones, digestion and diet, and the end of menstruation. Though prolapse is cited as a cause of sexual dysfunction, bothersome pelvic symptoms, and psychological stress, the discussion is nevertheless limited to a single paragraph.

Female incontinence, until recently, had often been granted only a chapter or two within broad guidebooks on both male and female incontinence. More recent guides have been more effectively focused on the female reader, although understanding and preventing the obstetrical origins of this disorder have been treated as an afterthought by virtually all of the existing incontinence guides. *The Urinary Incontinence Sourcebook* (Lowell House) outlines treatment alternatives using a practical, "soft textbook" style. Similarly, *Overcoming Incontinence: A Straightforward Guide to Your Options* by Mary Dierich and Felecia Froe (John Wiley & Sons) offers a checklist of therapeutic options ranging from office treatments to surgery. Recently, broader menopause guides have placed more empha-

sis on female incontinence, but readers will find
neither a comprehensive discussion of the available treatment alternatives nor any emphasis on
understanding their problem in the context of
their reproductive past. For example, Judith
Reichman's *I'm Too Young to Get Old* (Times Books)
covers incontinence in a short eight-page chapter
clearly intended to provide only a cursory
overview for what is described as a neglected and
underdiagnosed problem that "hasn't come out of
the closet." Yet, the exponentially increasing
number of specialists in this area, suddenly
exploding research budgets, and highly visible
advertising campaigns geared toward incontinent
women over the past few years would argue that
the closet is open.

Books addressing sexual dysfunction after
childbirth have mainly limited their scope to the
postpartum period and first year of motherhood.
Sheila Kitzinger's *The Year After Childbirth*

(Fireside, Simon & Schuster) discusses sexual
issues, but only through the postpartum period.
Judith Reichman's *I'm Not in the Mood* (Quill,
William Morrow) targets women in the perimenopause and alludes to the role of prolapse and
incontinence on diminished sexual function
("relaxation of our pelvic muscles is a price we
often pay for vaginal deliveries"). However,
these aspects are not integrated into the book's
self-help strategies, which focus on hormonal and
behavioral factors.

Ever Since I Had My Baby represents the first
book to explore these remarkably common disorders
together, offering a new perspective that illumi-
nates the full spectrum of childbirth-related
changes to the female body and their potential
consequences at many stages throughout a woman's
life. Arriving on the bookshelves before a mainstream urogynecology reference has yet to appear,
Ever Since I Had My Baby holds the promise of

capturing the market as the definitive layperson's "bible" for this exploding medical area—while offering a great deal more substance and thought provocation than the average self-help guidebook. The reader will treasure and turn these pages not only because they address neglected physical problems and provide the clearest and most comprehensive tools for ameliorating or preventing them, but also because the intimate health issues at the book's core are intertwined with one of the most unforgettable, defining, and wonderful experiences of her life: childbirth. Rarely has a "self-help" book, spanning from childbirth to menopause, addressed a female readership in such a fresh and intriguing way. *Ever Since I Had My Baby* will enter a truly unexplored niche within the expanding literary genre of women's health.

Goldberg/Proposal for *Ever Since I Had My Baby*   26

CONDENSED TABLE OF CONTENTS

Part One   **"What's Happening to Me Down There?"**

Preface   Beyond the Labor Room and After the Push

Chapter 1   Understanding Your Body After

             Childbirth

             Incontinence, Prolapse, and Other

             Common Changes

Chapter 2   Pelvic Anatomy During and After

             Vaginal Delivery

             Miracles Meet Reality

Part Two   **Treating Yourself**

Chapter 3   Exercises and Healthy Habits

             Home Treatments and Remedies

             for Incontinence, Prolapse, and

             Other Postobstetrical Problems

Chapter 4   Food, Drinks, Herbs, and Supplements

             The Impact of Diet and "Alternative"

             Self-Therapy

Goldberg/Proposal for *Ever Since I Had My Baby*   27

Chapter 5   Medications and Hormones

            Pills, Tablets, Creams, and Patches—

            How They Can Help

Chapter 6   Sex After Childbirth and Beyond

            Restoring Satisfaction, Sensation,

            and Self-Confidence

Chapter 7   Preventive Obstetrics

            Changing Childbirth, Present and

            Future

Part Three Professional Treatment

Chapter 8   Seeing the Doctor

            Where to Go, What to Expect

Chapter 9   Magnetic Chairs, Electric Probes,

                Pessaries, Pads, and More

            The Wide World of Nonsurgical Office

                Treatments and Simple Devices

Chapter 10 Surgery for Incontinence and Prolapse

            Choices, Effectiveness, Risks, and

            Recuperation

Afterword   The Stage Is All Yours

Navigating the Politics, Economics,

Culture, and Ethics of Childbirth

Appendix   Organizations, Online Resources, and

Support Groups

Query Letter and Proposal Sample #3

The query letter and proposal featured here are for the English cookbook mentioned in the Preface. It was the only book I wrote first, then tried to sell—without any luck. The query and proposal intrigued two agents in a twelve-year period, both of whom tried to sell the book; both were unsuccessful for the reasons speculated in the Preface.

Still, the query and proposal are pretty good. (Because the original proposal was written some dozen years ago, the author bio section was sorely out of date. It has been updated for this book.)

In addition to the proposal for *The English Good Food Cook Book*, I've written a spin-off proposal from one of the chapters—*Pub Grub*. That also has come close to acceptance but hasn't been picked up yet. It doesn't mean that another dozen years or so won't see success.

Dear _____:

It's been said the English are more concerned with
table manners than food, but that person probably
never dined in an English home. There are hundreds
of traditional English dishes with unusual and
intriguing names most Americans have never heard.
I am proposing an entertaining cookbook, informative enough to catch the attention of the average
or expert cook, the seasoned or armchair traveler,
and the discriminating gift buyer.

I have written a cookbook that's never been written before, *The English Good Food Cook Book*, a
collection of traditional English recipes. In
every bookstore you'll find dozens of bestselling
cookbooks on vegetarian cooking, gourmet cuisine,
and almost every ethnic variation imaginable,
except the one country from which many Americans
still trace their ancestry, England! What better
way to get in touch with your "roots"?

In addition to offering menus suggesting what to
serve with what and easy-to-follow recipes with
their historical background, my book will be a
pictorial journey through the kitchens and countryside of England.

Anyone who has ever spent any time in England
will appreciate this book for the fond memories
it will bring back of green idyllic scenery,
delicious wholesome food, and a quaint and
appealing culture. For those aspiring travelers,
my book will be an introduction to English food

and a way to vicariously experience the richness of England without ever having to leave home.

Each chapter will be highlighted by food-related photographs taken throughout England, depicting countryside picnic spots (lakes, forests, moors) and quaint eating establishments such as inns and pubs, along with eye-catching pub signs and unusual bed-and-breakfast hotels. Other regional points of interest such as traditional Beefeaters guarding the Tower of London, the white cliffs of Dover—home of the famous Dover sole—village market days, thatched-roof cottages with early-morning milk deliveries waiting on the doorstep, and traditional English teas in Victorian settings are all planned.

Rather than a high-gloss presentation, I am aiming for a peaceful, bucolic effect. England's rainy climate, misty moors, and foggy mornings lend themselves to photographs with subdued colors and lighting. Photographs of recipes can also be arranged, if so desired.

I am a freelance writer with articles in *Newsday*, *Fort Lauderdale News/Sun-Sentinel*, *Gulf Air's Inflight*, *What's On*, *International Living*, *Accent*, *AAA Going Places*, *Horseplay*, *Coins*, *Mainstream*, *Sign Craft*, *British Heritage*, and various other publications.

May I send you a detailed proposal, sample chapters, and published clips?

Sincerely,
Blythe Camenson
Blythe Camenson

Book Proposal:

The English Good Food Cook Book

by Blythe Camenson

INTRODUCTION

Is there such a thing, you might wonder, as English cuisine? Of course there is! And it's not just fish-and-chips, either.

Someone once said that England and America are two countries divided by a common language, and that person was right. On the surface, there might not seem to be many differences in cooking and food tastes between the two cousins (we both tend to like good old-fashioned roast beef for our Sunday dinners), but dig a little deeper and surprises abound. Common American words such as *biscuits*, *puddings*, *joints*, and *chips* take on a whole new meaning once translated into "English."

There are hundreds of traditional English dishes with unusual and intriguing names that most Americans have never heard of: toad in the hole, bubble and squeak, Dundee cake, and Lancashire hot pot, to name just a few. There are also more familiar dishes such as trifle and

Camenson/Proposal for *The English Good Food Cook Book*   2

Yorkshire pudding, but how many Americans know how to make a "proper" Yorkshire pudding or realize that it isn't really a "pudding" at all? And, more important, how easily can that information be found?

According to *Books in Print*, not too easily. There are very few British or English cookbooks on the market.

That gap is exactly what I plan to fill, by providing a novel and entertaining cookbook, attractive and informative enough to catch the attention of the average or expert cook, the seasoned or armchair traveler, and the discriminating gift buyer.

I have written a cookbook that's never been written before, *The English Good Food Cook Book*, a collection of traditional English recipes. In every bookstore you'll find dozens of bestselling cookbooks on vegetarian cooking, gourmet cuisine, and almost every ethnic variation imaginable,

Camenson/Proposal for *The English Good Food Cook Book*   3

except the one country from which many Americans still trace their ancestry, England!

What better way to get in touch with your "roots"? I have planned *The English Good Food Cook Book* to be more than just another cookbook. In addition to offering menus suggesting what goes with what and easy-to-follow recipes with historical background, my book is a pictorial journey through the kitchens and countryside of England.

THE MARKET

Because of *The English Good Food Cook Book*'s quality photographs, tempting recipes, and information on traditions and lifestyle, I believe it will attract a wide audience. The large number of Anglo-Americans proud of their heritage will be drawn to this cookbook to keep as a highly valued heirloom. Anyone who has ever spent any time in England will appreciate this book for the fond memories it will bring back of green idyllic scenery, delicious wholesome food, and a quaint and appealing culture. For those aspiring travelers, my book will be an introduction to English food and a way to vicariously experience the richness of England without ever having to leave home.

Of course, anyone who likes to cook and has a family to feed or friends to entertain will enjoy bringing something new to the table. *The English Good Food Cook Book* will also make the perfect gift, a gift that won't have to be hidden away in the kitchen. My book will be beautiful enough to sit proudly beside any other coffee-table production, and it will put an end to the search for something special and different to serve by opening up for Americans an, as yet, unexplored area of cooking.

I believe that my cookbook will be a successful venture because good cookbooks have a long shelf life. Unless based on a passing food fad or trend, they rarely date themselves. A good recipe will always be a good recipe. A friend recently confessed that, in addition to her library of current cookbooks, she still uses the one her mother passed down to her, a *Good Housekeeping* cookbook, circa 1945.

English recipes have also withstood the passage of time, handed down from generation to generation. *The English Good Food Cook Book* contains time-honored, traditional recipes that could join other classic cookbooks. Cookbook lovers cherish their cookbooks. They make excellent gifts and serve as handy reference tools in practically every kitchen in America.

FORMAT

Another friend showed me a twenty-year-old travel guide that claimed English food was bland and boring. The writer had probably visited England but obviously had never eaten in an English home!

It's true that Britain is not noted for its restaurants; when most English people eat out, they opt for ethnic meals or stick to traditional fish-and-chips shops. But when a good English meal is desired, the best place to eat is at home!

England is a country famous for rich dairy products (cream so thick it doesn't need to be whipped), tender beef, and fresh produce. English home cooks serve only the very best quality.

The English Good Food Cook Book will introduce the reader to all the traditional English dishes, the old standard favorites as well as unfamiliar but tried-and-tested recipes. There are more than 120 recipes included in this book. An informative introduction to each chapter gives background on the recipes, tells for which special occasion they are commonly used, and provides easy-to-follow instructions for preparation. Several of the chapters are presented in menu format, suggesting what dishes to serve with what.

Camenson/Proposal for *The English Good Food Cook Book*   7

Each chapter will be highlighted by food-related photographs taken throughout England, depicting countryside picnic spots (lakes, forests, moors) and quaint eating establishments such as inns and pubs, along with eye-catching pub signs and unusual bed-and-breakfast hotels. Other regional points of interest such as traditional Beefeaters guarding the Tower of London, the white cliffs of Dover—home of the famous Dover sole—village market days, thatched-roof cottages with early-morning milk deliveries waiting on the doorstep, and Victorian tea settings are all planned.

Rather than a high-gloss, garish presentation, I am aiming for a peaceful, bucolic effect. England's rainy climate, misty moors, and foggy mornings lend themselves to photographs with muted and subdued colors and lighting. Photographs of particularly unusual recipes can also be arranged, if so desired.

Camenson/Proposal for *The English Good Food Cook Book* 8

To make this cookbook completely effortless to use, all English recipes are translated into "American," giving standard familiar weights and measures. For English ingredients difficult to find in America, appropriate substitutes are suggested.

The book contains ten chapters with headings such as The English Breakfast, Pub Grub, English Country Picnics, Afternoon Tea, and Christmas Puddings.

Each chapter of the book, in addition to the photographic spread, includes background information on the dishes or regions from which they originate, offers a variety of menus, and presents easy-to-follow recipes. The book also contains an introduction, a table of contents, a glossary, and an index.

THE AUTHOR

Blythe Camenson has a B.A. in English and psychology and a master's degree in education. She has been living in the Middle East since 1982 working

Camenson/Proposal for *The English Good Food Cook Book*   9

with British expatriates and basing herself in London during her long summer leaves. She is a freelance writer with articles in *British Heritage*, *Newsday* (Travel), *Fort Lauderdale News/Sun-Sentinel* (Travel), *Gulf Air's Inflight*, *What's On*, *Treasure*, and various other publications.

DELIVERY

The completed manuscript can be sent to you at your request.

CHAPTER SUMMARY

The summary that follows delineates each chapter's focus, gives a sample menu, and provides a brief look at some of the historical information contained in the completed book.

Chapter 1: The English Breakfast

W. Somerset Maugham once said, "To eat well in England you should have breakfast three times a day." Of course, we know he meant that he was so taken with the English breakfast that he lost all interest in other meals. In later chapters, I will show how much Maugham missed out on, but in this chapter the focus is on the meal Britons believe to be the most important.

An English breakfast is traditionally large and filling and taken for granted as each person's due. Breakfast is generally included as a matter of course in the price of a hotel room in England, thus generating the name of the popular establishments called "bed-and-breakfasts."

This chapter includes photographs of some of the quainter B&Bs and country inns, as well as several different menus for a traditional English breakfast and recipes and instructions for preparing homemade jams and marmalade and unfamiliar dishes such as kedgeree and "ox eye eggs."

Camenson/Proposal for *The English Good Food Cook Book* 11

Sample Menu

Eggs in potato nests

English bacon and kidneys

Grilled tomatoes

Kedgeree

Marmalade and jam

Chapter 2: Pub Grub

The pub (short for public house) is a British
institution; every neighborhood and business dis-
trict boasts at least one of these quaint, comfortable gathering places. Ask any Englishman to
tell you about his "local" and he'll probably
regale you with colorful tales of the lively
atmosphere, friendly competition (darts, snooker,
quiz nights), and stomach-warming fare.

This chapter takes the reader on a short photographic tour of some popular locals and, in
addition to background information on some of the

Camenson/Proposal for *The English Good Food Cook Book* 12

dishes (e.g., 91,000 pork pies were consumed during Queen Victoria's ten-day jubilee in 1887), provides complete recipes for the lunchtime meals traditionally offered.

Bill of Fayre

Ploughman's lunch

Pork pies

Steak, kidney, and oyster pudding

Lancashire hot pot

Steak and kidney pie

Cottage pie

Chapter 3: Afternoon Tea

Tea is to Britain what chicken soup is to America, a panacea for any problem. In the middle of a crisis that the author personally witnessed (a woman was mugged), each person standing by was assigned a specific task to help: get a blanket,

Camenson/Proposal for *The English Good Food Cook Book* 13

call an ambulance, notify the police, and put on a pot of tea!

Just as the Japanese take great pride in their honored tea ceremonies, so do the British. Included in this chapter are step-by-step instructions for making a "proper" pot of tea, recipes for the "turn out" traditionally served to accompany it, and a brief history of the origin of the "afternoon tea."

Tea and Turn Out

Tea

Swirled sandwiches

Scones

Rock cakes

Hot-cross buns

Dundee cake

Camenson/Proposal for *The English Good Food Cook Book* 14

Chapter 4: Sunday Dinner

Usually served midday, this is the meal the English pull out all the stops for. Yorkshire pudding, a batter-based biscuit, is the Sunday roast's usual accompaniment. Originally, the working classes in northern England used Yorkshire pudding as an inexpensive food to fatten up a skimpy dinner table. Over the last two hundred years or so, it has grown in popularity and stretched across class barriers to become a dish Britons are proud of. It can be served as an appetizer or to complement the Sunday dinner's main course.

Trifle is traditionally served on Sundays for dessert. Oliver Wendell Holmes described it as "That most wonderful object of domestic art called trifle . . . with its charming confusion of cream and cake and almonds and jam and jelly and wine and cinnamon and froth."

Camenson/Proposal for *The English Good Food Cook Book* 15

Sample Menu

Roast prime rib of beef

Yorkshire pudding

Roast potatoes

Brussels sprouts with almonds

Sherry trifle

Chapter 5: Family Dinner

English women are an equal part of the workforce
and are both working wives and mothers. The evening meal, served around six o'clock, is the one
time of the day when the whole family can take
"tea" together. Meals are generally simple and
easy to prepare, saving the bigger dinners and
afternoon teas for the weekends.

Sample Menu

Hindle Wakes

Celery rice

Bread and butter pudding

Chapter 6: St. Valentine's Day Romantic Dinners for Two

Englishmen have somehow earned a reputation (ill-deserved) of being unromantic. Not so! St. Valentine's Day in England is just one of the many occasions when lovers express their feelings for each other, and the everyday frozen peas and chips are put aside in favor of more gourmet cuisine.

This chapter provides menus and recipes for those special candlelit dinners for two.

Sample Menu

Salmon mousse

Shrewsbury lamb noisettes

Stuffed artichokes

Creamed potatoes

Burnt cream

Camenson/Proposal for *The English Good Food Cook Book* 17

Chapter 7: English Country Picnics

England is filled with parks, forests, lakes, and moors. The rainy climate has provided numerous idyllic green spots perfect for picnicking. The hardy English often have to wait a long time for a sunny day, but when one finally appears, they don't hesitate to spread out a blanket and unpack a picnic hamper.

A photographic display of the English countryside accompanies the menus and recipes for a variety of picnic meals.

Sample Menu

Potted crab

Cornish pasties

Scotch eggs

Summer pudding

Camenson/Proposal for *The English Good Food Cook Book* 18

Chapter 8: Children's Fayre

Guy Fawkes Night, Children's Tea Parties,

Shrove Tuesday

Light up the bonfire, get out your woolies, and set the table with hearty and bone-warming fayre for the wee ones. This chapter tells the story of Guy Fawkes Night, England's closest equivalent to the American Halloween. It also explains the traditional food (pancakes) and festivities for Shrove Tuesday and gives menus and recipes for these events, as well as children's tea parties.

Sample Menu

Scotch broth

Toad in the hole

Potatoes in jackets with cheese

Jolly good fudge

Apple fool

Camenson/Proposal for *The English Good Food Cook Book* 19

Chapter 9: The Earl of Sandwich

No book on English cooking would be complete without a section on sandwiches, since one of Britain's own is credited with their invention. This chapter gives background on the Fourth Earl of Sandwich, noted as an unsavory, corrupt character who preferred gambling to eating and thus came up with the sandwich as a convenient way to eat without having to leave the gaming table. Open sandwiches, sandwich fillings, and bread recipes are included in this chapter.

Samples

Open sandwiches: Lancashire rarebit,

Lincolnshire Haslet

Sandwich fillings

Homemade breads: milkloaf, English tea bread,

granary loaf

Camenson/Proposal for *The English Good Food Cook Book* 20

Chapter 10: Christmas Puddings

Every Western country has its own way to celebrate Christmas, though many traditions overlap country borders. England and America share many of the same customs, and December 25 dinner tables on both sides of the Atlantic look remarkably similar, except when it comes to desserts!

Chocolate holly-decorated Yule logs and traditional mince pies delight every dinner guest, whether youngster or adult. This chapter contains recipes for a variety of Christmas "puddings" and beverages.

Samples

Yule log

Plum pudding

Twelfth Night cake

Wassail

Mince pies

Mulled wine

Money and Contracts

"Writing is the hardest way of earning a living, with the possible exception of wrestling alligators."

—Olin Miller

MANY NEW WRITERS approach writing as an art. Others sustain themselves with fantasies of fame and riches. When the good news of an acceptance finally does arrive (and with persistence, hard work, good writing and research, market savvy, and a little luck, it will), the bubble can burst for both groups. Seasoned writers understand that writing is more business than art. And they know that most writers never see the glory of the bestseller list or the commensurate advance or royalty check.

"There is probably no other trade in which there is so little relationship between profits and actual value, or into which sheer chance so largely enters," says Kathleen O'Brien, an English writer, quoted in *Author! Author!*

"Writers rarely become rich and famous because of the quality of their work," said the late Gary Provost, writer and teacher, as quoted in an issue of *Writer's Digest* some years ago. "They become rich and famous because of the nature of their work."

A senior manager in the contracts department for a major trade book publisher based in New York says, "New authors in particular should have realistic expectations regarding the financial and other terms of their contracts. Not many authors are (or will be) a Stephen Covey or a Stephen Ambrose, and authors should not have delusions of grandeur regarding in what manner they expect their work to be marketed or sold, or what royalties or other considerations they should be entitled to receive."

Unfortunately, that attitude is more the norm than the exception. A new writer's education usually starts when he or she is presented with the first advance offer and then the contract.

Advances

One of the most exciting things to happen in this industry for a first-time author is to be offered his or her first advance. One of the most exciting—and often the most disappointing.

Except for a select few, advances for a first book (and even subsequent ones) are rarely glamorous. The good news, however, is that there is no such thing as a typical advance. Advances can range from $1,000 to $1 million. And there's no reason a new book couldn't command an advance at the higher end of the scale.

Here are the factors that can affect the size of an advance:

- The subject matter
- Originality (how new and different the book is)
- The excitement the idea generates within a publishing house
- The competition among publishers to acquire the project
- The size of the publisher's budget (which can be miraculously increased when excitement has been generated)
- Estimate of first-year earnings
- The particular audience for the book (Are they known big spenders?)
- Author credentials
- Presentation of the idea in a great proposal
- Good agenting (good negotiating)
- Luck

Wise Words

The freelance writer is a man who is paid per piece or per word or perhaps.

—Robert Benchley

Contemporary Books editor Denise Betts sheds some light on the subject: "Advances in general may be modest if the writer isn't well known in his or her field. Other considerations are the subject matter—some categories are known to bring in less money than others—and the market for the book.

"For example, the professional wrestling fan base is huge, and they are known to spend a lot of money on anything relating to the sport and the characters involved in the sport. It's no wonder that Mankind Mick Foley and The Rock's biographies were on the *New York Times* bestseller lists. If you have a solid project catering to that audience, you may be able to negotiate a higher advance.

"Keep in mind, however, that publishers determine the level of advances based on a variety of factors, so there's a limit on how high their offer will be. Also, this is just money up-front, a gesture of good faith that the book will earn out and then go on to make money for the publisher and the author through royalties throughout the life of the book."

Agent-Author Contracts

There is a legal side to the profession of writing. Whenever there's some sort of legal relationship into which two or more parties enter, a contract is usually part of the deal. You may sign your first contract when you find an agent. Some agents use formal contracts; some send new clients a letter of agreement; some wait until they've made a sale and then attach an addendum to the book contract the publisher offers.

When looking over the contract the agent offers you, make sure the contract protects your interests as well as the agent's and has a clause for you to dissolve the relationship, if it should come to that.

Here are some other terms to look for in your agent-author contract:

- **Material the agent will represent.** Make sure you can contract with your new agent on a book-by-book basis. Perhaps this is your first nonfiction book, but you've built up a successful career for yourself writing romance novels, too. You've placed these yourself, and you don't want to start having to suddenly pay a commission to an agent who had nothing to do with these book deals.
- **Commission percentages.** Make sure the agent's commission is specified in the contract. Most take 15 percent for domestic sales and 20 percent for foreign rights and film rights.
- **Reimbursable expenses.** Discuss with the agent in advance what expenses you will be expected to pay. Some charge for faxes and long-distance calls, messenger services, and photocopying. Some agents will deduct these expenses when they make a sale for you; others want an amount up front to hold on account. Still others will charge you as the expense comes up. Be sure to set a limit to how much you will be asked to pay.

When It's Time to Fire Your Agent

You haven't heard from your agent in a couple of weeks. Is it time to fire her? No. It's been six months and he hasn't sold your book yet. Is it time to fire him? No. It's been one year. No sales, and for the past few months, you haven't heard back from her, in spite of your repeated attempts to contact her. Is it time to fire her? Probably.

In Chapter 3, we discussed what to expect from your agent. If your agent isn't delivering, it might be time to move on. Here are three major warning signs:

- Your agent's initial enthusiasm for your project has waned. Now he's saying that no one is interested.
- She's not able to document where she's sent your proposal. She doesn't send you any correspondence from editors. All those rejections but none in writing make you suspicious.
- He won't return your calls or E-mails. He seems to have slipped into a black void.

When it's time to fire your agent, reread the contract you signed. Follow the provisions noted in the termination clause. If she wants thirty days' written notice sent by registered mail, then you must comply.

When you send your letter terminating your agent-client relationship, remember not to burn any bridges. The world of publishing is a small one and word gets around about hostile writers. (The word also gets around about ineffective agents, so don't worry about that.)

Make sure to instruct your soon-to-be-former agent not to submit any more proposals or manuscripts on your behalf. Ask that all material be returned to you. Close the letter by thanking her for her work on your behalf, then move on.

You can look for a new agent or go it solo. And when that lucky day arrives and you receive an offer for your proposed book, you'll be given another type of contract—a book contract.

Book Contracts

You're a writer, not a lawyer. Your first book contract arrives and you can't make heads or tails of it. Here's where an agent comes in handy. If you don't have one, you might go look for one now. (It's much easier finding an agent when you already have a contract. Some agents will charge you a one-time fee to go over the contract with you. Others, if they negotiate for you with your publisher, will expect the full commission on your advance and future sales. They might, however, land you an advance and royalty percentage higher than what you could for yourself.)

If you ask your new editor whether you need an agent, you may be assured you're doing fine without one, that an agent won't get any more

---

Wise Words

I love being a writer. What I can't stand is the paperwork.

—Peter De Vries

money, that the terms are boilerplate and not negotiable. This isn't necessarily true. Discuss this with an agent or a publishing law attorney.

"At one level, publishing contracts are deceptively simple," says publishing law attorney Lloyd J. Jassin. "In exchange for an advance against royalties, the author grants the publisher the exclusive right to publish her work in book form. The terms are set down in a 'standard' author-publisher agreement. Simple on its face. Complicated in fact, since there is no such thing as a standard author-publisher agreement.

"Some of the key deal points in a publishing contract are the grant of rights, manuscript delivery, advance, royalty, and accounting provisions. The contract should clearly specify what rights are being granted. Is the grant for both hardcover and trade paperback versions? Does it extend to mass market paperbacks? Audio books? E-books? How do you define E-books? The scope of rights granted is usually discussed when the publishing agreement is first negotiated. In trade publishing, authors generally retain performance rights (motion picture, TV, and radio) and merchandising rights. However, many publishers will try to grab those rights. If an agent represents you, she might seek to retain foreign translation and first serial rights."

Publishing law attorney Sara Goodman says, "Every writer should expect to extend warranties and indemnities to his publisher. The publisher needs to know that the writer has the right to enter into the contract (i.e., there are no employment agreements, no confidentiality agreements, no prior publishing agreements, or any other agreements previously entered into that prohibit the writer from writing and delivering the book in question).

"In addition, the writer should expect to promise the publisher that it won't get sued for publishing the book. Usually these promises take the form of warranties about libel, invasion of privacy, and copyright infringement.

"Warranties are essentially promises from the writer to the publisher, guaranteeing certain conditions to the publisher and assuring the publisher that it can rely on those promises and publish the work without fear of liability. The writer extends 'indemnities,' further assuring the publisher that he will defend the publisher if it turns out that he breaks his promises. These are all standard terms in any publishing agreement."

A senior manager in the contracts department for a major New York–based trade book publisher confirms, "The basic terms, such as warranties/indemnity and accounting procedures (which are impractical to vary from author to author) are essentially nonnegotiable. There are many clauses for which we may change some of the details, but not the fundamentals. In

---

Wise Words

Write without pay until somebody offers to pay you. If nobody offers within three years, sawing wood is what you were intended for.

—Mark Twain

---

addition, we have many standard variations for other parts of the contract (such as the noncompete), but we generally do not depart from our standard variations."

Royalties

The first royalty check you'll receive is the advance; an advance comes under the category of royalties. An advance is usually an estimate of how much money the publisher thinks the book will earn in its first year in print. You won't get another royalty check until the book has sold enough to earn back its advance. In some instances that might happen in the first sales period. Or, if the advance was large and the sales are slow, it could take a year or more.

It varies from publisher to publisher, but royalty checks and sales statements are generally issued twice a year and cover the previous sales period. "Advances are usually paid in installments," says Lloyd Jassin. "Generally, half on signing, the balance on the publisher's acceptance of your completed manuscript. Keep in mind that royalties and other payments to the author can vary significantly. For hardcover books, royalties generally rise in steps, based on the number of copies actually sold. Traditionally, authors receive 10 percent of the suggested retail price on the first five thousand hardcover copies sold, 12.5 percent on the next five thousand, and 15 percent after that. Trade paperback royalties are usually lower than hardcover royalties, generally between 6 percent and 8 percent, sometimes rising to 10 percent.

"But beware! Not all publishers base their royalties on the retail price of the book. If your royalty is based on the 'net' price of the book, assuming an average discount of 50 percent, a net royalty of 10 percent is the same as 5 percent of list.

"In an author-friendly contract, it is not uncommon for an author to receive 75 percent to 85 percent of the income from foreign rights sales. Low-normal might be 50 percent of what the publisher receives from the licensing of foreign translation rights.

"There are a number of reduced royalty clauses that show up in book contracts today. Some of these clauses—unless modified—can dramatically reduce your royalty check." One of these is the royalty pool (discussed under Contractual Pitfalls).

Flat Fees

Some book publishers will offer you a flat fee instead of an advance against royalties. The flat fee (also known as work for hire) might be higher than the advance would have been on a royalty contract, but that will be all the money you'll get for that particular book. If it goes on to be a bestseller, you're out of luck. If it doesn't sell many copies, then you were better off with the flat fee.

Sometimes a work-for-hire contract will not allow the writer to keep the copyright in his or her name. Book packagers often work this way. With a flat-fee contract, you have to weigh the advantages and disadvantages.

Contractual Pitfalls

A good agent or publishing law attorney will be very familiar with publisher boilerplate contracts and will know what can be negotiated and what can't. Here are some things to look out for, according to publishing law attorney Lloyd Jassin.

"An important clause is the satisfactory manuscript clause. The satisfactory manuscript clause gives your publisher the option to accept or reject your manuscript if it is not 'satisfactory.' Since payment of your advance is tied to acceptance, how this clause is drafted is critical. From an author's point of view, a good acceptance clause obligates your publisher to accept or reject your manuscript within x days of delivery. If your publisher rejects the manuscript, it should explain what it would take to make it acceptable and allow you a period of thirty to sixty days within which to resubmit the manuscript.

"There are a number of important accounting issues—many of them negotiable, provided you know what to ask for. Your book, if it doesn't sell through, can be returned to your publisher for credit. To protect themselves, publishers withhold a percentage of your royalties, so the house doesn't pay you for books that are later returned. This is known as a 'reserve for returns' clause. You should try to limit the amount withheld. While some publishers hold on to the reserve for a limited period, others liquidate only when the book goes out of print. That is unfair."

Author Rick Hautala has published more than a dozen books. "The setting for most hocus-pocus is the reserves against returns clause," he warns. "Publishers almost never specify what the percentage taken is. And they never specify how long they'll hold the reserve. The publisher will tell you the percentage varies, but they never say based on what. (Some writers think publishers manipulate the reserves just to keep a book from earning out its advance.) It's nothing but an interest-free loan to your publisher."

"The frequency of statements and the form they are received in is important, too," says Lloyd Jassin. "Some contracts don't contain an audit clause. Without an audit clause, unless you sue your publisher, they aren't going to open their books."

Late freelance writer Vanda Sendzimir cautioned, "Also avoid the twelve-month look-back clause. This prevents you from reviewing their accounting beyond one year back. By the time you get your second statement, eighteen months to two years may have gone by.

"Also avoid the gag clause. You can audit their books, but you can't publicize the results. Writers' organizations might help with your audit, but not if they can't reveal the numbers at the end."

"How the term *out of print* is defined is also important," says Lloyd Jassin. "When a book goes out of print, the author is able to recapture her rights. Most contracts were drafted before the arrival of 'print on demand' technology. If a book is stored electronically—as bits and bytes—it need never go 'OP.' From an author's point of view, the reversion of rights should be tied to the sale of a minimum number of royalty-bearing copies.

"Other important clauses are the 'competing book' and 'revised edition' clause. If you plan to write other books, or if your book is successful, these clauses—unless modified—could be harmful.

"Some of these clauses—for example, option, competing book, and revised edition clauses—are highly negotiable. A quick word about option clauses: if you don't believe a bad deal today won't haunt you tomorrow, look at a standard option clause. Most boilerplate clauses require you to deliver a finished manuscript of your next work to your publisher for their consideration. If the publisher likes the work, the terms of option might be on the same terms as your first book. Many publishers will allow you to strike the option clause in its entirety. Others will allow you to limit it in a number of ways. For example, the author need only submit a sample chapter. Perhaps, the option on the 'next' book only applies to the author's next mystery novel (not how-to book). Instead of the option being on the same terms as the first book, your publisher might agree to an exclusive thirty-day period in which to negotiate the terms of your next book contract."

How you negotiate royalties will also affect you now and down the road. *Make sure* your contract doesn't insist on joint accounting or a royalty pool, said Vanda Sendzimir. "If you are signing up for more than one book with a single publisher, try to get your titles accounted for separately. If your first book doesn't earn out its advance, they'll keep money from the royalties of your second book. That means that a book that is selling well pays the publisher for a book that isn't. It also means that you are taking the risk, not the publisher. You might never see a royalty check that way. And sometimes the royalty statement won't even reflect joint accounting." (Joint accounting is often used for multibook deals, and if the advance goes over six figures, you won't be able to avoid it.)

Royalty Statements

Let's start off with a fair royalty statement. Legitimate publishers don't normally intend to confuse, mislead, or cheat their writers. They wouldn't still be in business if they did. But if you've never seen a royalty statement, ask a published friend to share one of his or hers. You can also contact your local writers' groups to find a statement. Be prepared. It will look like Greek, even though your publisher isn't in Athens.

Vanda Sendzimir wrote in her article "Royalty Statements: Gospel or Gobbledygook?" that "Royalty statements can, occasionally, lie. Sometimes they mislead, misrepresent, or just plain mess up the figures. Most authors don't have the knowledge, time, or patience to decipher them, and unfortunately many agents don't either."

"Ultimately, you can't verify your royalty statements," says Phil Mattera, a veteran book grievance officer for the National Writers Union (NWU). "But you can reduce the odds that you're being grossly cheated."

Vanda Sendzimir wrote, "There are two problems that can arise within a royalty statement: the sales figures are accurate but the way they're calculated or categorized is incorrect, or else the numbers are just plain wrong. How to know?

"First, look at the numbers critically. Is the math right? Is everything on there that should be? Author Victoria Thompson noticed on one of her royalty statements that there was much less on the bottom line than she expected. She studied the statement and realized they'd left off book club sales.

"Is your book on the bestseller list but the royalty figures are mysteriously low? Author Mike Echols says he got suspicious when the first royalty statement for his mass market true crime book said sales were over 20,000, but 'the book was everywhere—bookstores, drugstores, supermarkets. The figures should have been much higher.' He started investigating. He called bookstores, wholesalers, and retail outlets to ask for sales figures on his book.

"If your suspicions are raised but you're not a private eye, then what? Try asking your editor how your book is doing; most publishers do internal monthly reports, so your editor should have some idea. A call to the royalty or accounting department may sort things out. Simple mistakes can be corrected."

Phil Mattera suggests that you ask your publisher for the Reconciliation to Print report. This report is like the publisher's own audit about what's happening with the book: number of books printed, shipped, defective, destroyed, in stock, and so on.

Make a request that your royalty statements (or material accompanying them) contain lots of information, such as numbers of copies sold, list price of copies sold, royalty rate, amount of reserves held against returns, royalties to the publisher from the licensing agreements, itemized deductions, and so on.

And if all else fails, get help.

Help Is Available

You're a writer; you're not expected to be an accountant or a lawyer. But you are ultimately responsible for what you sign. Educate yourself and get help—it's available. If you have an agent, she should be able to make calls on your behalf and should be in a better position to discover royalty statement errors, especially if she has several authors with the same house.

The Authors Guild will help you draft a letter to your publisher and refer you to an auditor in New York.

The National Writers Union will review your royalty statements and represent you as a grievant if the dispute gets that far. The NWU is also drafting a standardized royalty statement for the industry.

The American Society of Journalists and Authors (ASJA) website also gives information on contracts, electronic rights, and copyright to the general public. The website for this information is asja.org/cwpage.htm (See Appendix A for additional contact details.)

The best advice for contracts and royalty statements is to educate yourself. Know what they do say and know what they should say. If you're one of the lucky 20 to 30 percent of writers who earn out their advance, don't let a simple accounting error or worse deprive you of your hard-won gains.

Who Does the Index?

Most nonfiction books include an index as part of the back matter. Some publishers, as a matter of course, contract this job out to a freelancer—and charge that fee to you. You might want to negotiate removing that fee. If that doesn't work, offer to do the index yourself and earn an additional fee. Your word processing program most likely has a feature to index automatically the terms you designate.

Advice from Two Publishing Law Attorneys

Lloyd J. Jassin

"Authors have a larger stake in the success or failure of their book than their publisher. Unless you've received a large advance, there's no guarantee your publisher will be very aggressive in promoting your book. In fact, most publishers rely primarily on the author's ability to generate publicity and promotion—spending very little on the book beyond the advance and actual manufacturing costs. In short, your job doesn't end when you deliver your manuscript.

"Authors should also be aware that the success or failure of their book is determined many months before actual publication. Publications such as *Publishers Weekly, Library Journal*, and *Booklist* are 'advance' review media. Their editorial deadlines close several months before your book is physically available. Include a provision in your contract that requires your publisher to send

Contract Checklist

To make things a little bit easier when negotiating your contract, keep this checklist handy.

Be careful with or avoid

- Competing book clause
- Revised edition clause
- Royalty pool or joint accounting
- Satisfactory manuscript clause
- Giving away all rights
- Royalty based on net price as opposed to retail price
- Reserve for returns clause (the dollar amount and the time limit)
- Twelve-month look-back clause
- Gag clause
- Definition of *out of print*
- Option on next book clause

Negotiate into your contract

- Audit provision
- Author-friendly royalty statement (contains all relevant information)
- A sufficient number of author copies (ten to twenty)
- Expenses incurred while writing the book (travel, phone, payment for permissions, and so on)
- How to handle disputes
- Responsibility for the index

bound galleys or uncorrected proofs to these publications. Because of the expense involved—especially for nonfiction works—some publishers skip this step.

"Of particular importance for nonfiction authors is getting the book in the hands of reviewers at specialized publications. Therefore, it pays to ask your publisher to set aside review copies for reviewers, journalists, and opinion leaders you have personal relations with. Make this a contractual obligation."

For more information, visit Lloyd Jassin's website at copylaw.com.

Sara Goodman

"The most important thing to understand about publishing contracts is that you, the owner of the copyright in your writing, are granting the publisher the right to copy and sell your original work. The publisher has no rights until you specify what those rights are in the contract. In most publishing contracts, the writer retains his copyright but grants the publisher certain specified rights that his copyright includes—such as the exclusive right to publish the book in certain formats and territories (hardcover, softcover, movie, magazine serial excerpt, audio, video, foreign language, electronic, Internet, etc.). No contract is the same. Some writers retain certain rights because the publisher isn't interested in marketing those rights. Some writers feel that they can better handle certain rights. Usually the writer gets a royalty (either a percentage of the cover price or a percentage of what the publisher actually receives from booksellers) on each copy sold from the main publication of the work. If the book has a life beyond the main book itself (for example, a movie, a Spanish translation, a magazine excerpt), the publisher and writer will also split the income that is generated from the sale of those subsidiary rights. (Subsidiary rights are the rights beyond the main book rights.) Different rights sales yield different splits, but many rights split on a fifty-fifty basis.

"Other standard terms will include delivery, acceptability or rejection of the manuscript, how to handle disputes, options, and noncompete clauses.

"Avoid entanglements for future books by way of strangulating option clauses. If everyone gets along well after publication of Book #1, there's always room to negotiate a contract for Book #2.

"Also, keep a written record of correspondence with the publisher, even if the editor seems like the warmest, most friendly person in the world. If the publisher decides to cancel the book, the writer needs to be able to persuasively argue his entitlement to monies not yet paid if the situation warrants such an entitlement.

"Don't be afraid to ask lots of questions of the publisher. No question is stupid, and it's best to understand what actually happens in the publishing world. It's not at all a hostile world."

6

Researching and Writing
Your Nonfiction Book

*"The art of writing is the art of applying the seat of the pants
to the seat of the chair."*

—Mary Heaton Vorse

YOU'VE SOLD YOUR book and the contract has been signed, sealed, and delivered. You've deposited the check for the first half of your advance (it will probably clear; no need to worry about that). Now it's time to get down to the business at hand—writing your book.

If the reality of having to write an entire book settles in and starts to overwhelm you, don't let it. In this chapter you'll learn how to break your book down into manageable chunks you can work on—one chunk at a time.

But even before you begin to write, there's something else you must do first.

The Research You'll Need

Unless you are an expert and have been working with or teaching the material about which you plan to write for years, it's unlikely you'll be able to throw this book together off the top of your head. Most nonfiction writers must research their material. Even memoir writers must verify dates and other facts.

The type of information you'll need will vary depending on the subject of your book, but you'll most likely need some statistics and some sources to provide quotes, full interviews, case studies, or anecdotes.

You'll also need to find the resources you want to include in your appendices. Perhaps you'll be recommending books or periodicals, or you'll be listing professional associations. You'll need to locate accurate and up-to-date information for such resources.

These days the Internet is the best vehicle for research, hands down. Fire up your favorite search engine, type in a few key words, and you're off. Copy and paste addresses and URLs as needed.

Make sure, though, not to copy full pages of texts. Most websites are copyrighted, and the material is not just there for the taking. Always contact the website owner for permission if you'd like to quote any material.

If you don't find the information you need at the different websites, don't forget to use the "Contact Us" link most websites provide. Your query might lead you to just the information you're seeking.

Sample Internet Search

Let's say you're writing a book on divorce and you need some interesting statistics. How many divorces are obtained each year? Who instigates the divorce? What are the most common grounds for divorce? And so on. You go to a search engine and type in the key words *divorce*, *figures*, and *statistics*. The first hit you get says Divorce: Facts, Figures, and Consequences. You click on the link and get taken to a URL registered to a psychologist who has posted her paper on the subject at her university's website. The psychologist is from England and she compares many British statistics to those for the United States. You can use the same statistics, as long as you cite where they were found. This would also be the perfect person to quote in your book. E-mail her with the paragraphs of her paper that interest you and ask for permission

---

Wise Words

The greatest part of a writer's time is spent in reading; in order to write, a man will turn over half a library to make one book.

—Samuel Johnson

---

to use them. Offer her a complimentary copy of the book if you use her material. (Check with your publisher before you make such an offer. If the publisher isn't willing to send out a number of comp copies, the cost to you could become prohibitive. You don't need to offer the book in thanks—do so only if it's feasible.)

You're finished at this site, so you click your back button and return to the hits the search engine found for you. Another link says Divorce Statistics Available Free from State Governments. At that site you can read some sample statistics for the state of Texas and find out how to get other figures for other states. You also learn that each state has a Vital Statistics Department.

Is there a federal branch as well? Try another search. Type in key words such as *federal statistics bureau* or *office* and you come up with several thousand hits—many in overseas countries. Narrow your search and type in *U.S. federal statistics office* or *bureau*. You'll find links to offices such as the following:

- U.S. Census Bureau (the official resource for social, demographic, and economic statistics, which includes news releases, a subscription service, and a search facility)
- U.S. Department of Education (research and statistics)
- U.S. Government Information (a directory of online resources that provides a range of information, including legislation and standards)
- U.S. Bureau of Transportation Statistics: Port of Entries (location of the ports of entry on all U.S. land borders, and statistics on the amount of traffic through each of them)

- Bureau of Justice Statistics' Drugs and Crime Page (information, statistics, and publications about drugs and crime in the United States)
- Bureau of Labor Statistics (a good site with a table providing an overview of the economy and links to programs and surveys, research papers, and regional information)

It's easy to get lost in cyberspace, with one link leading to another leading to another. Try to keep your search organized by bookmarking the ones you think you'll want to revisit.

Here are some general research URLs to help you out. Your own search will no doubt lead you to many more:

For Speakers/Interviews/Quotes

America Online Speakers Bureau (offers professional speakers)
corp.aol.com/speakbureau/speakersbureau.html

The London Speaker Bureau (providing business, motivational, and after-dinner speakers)
londonspeakerbureau.co.uk

MJM Speakers' Bureau (representing professional speakers, trainers, humorists, entertainers, and celebrities from diverse backgrounds)
mjmspeakers.com

KM Connections—Quotes by "Experts" (quotes and comments from scientific experts)
runestone.org/kmcnnct.html

TPCN—Great Quotations (Quotes) to Inspire and Motivate You (quotations on every subject under the sun)
cyber-nation.com/victory/quotations

Organizing Your Research

You've collected your research and now it's time to organize it. Begin by creating a file on your computer for each chapter you'll write. Follow the sample table of contents from your proposal. Then create a file for any additional sections of your book, as needed:

Acknowledgments
Dedication
About the author
Contents
Foreword
Introduction
Appendix A
Appendix B
Appendix C
Bibliography

Copy and paste all relevant research into the file for each chapter or section, including appendices.

You can also copy and paste your chapter summaries from your proposal and the outline from your sample table of contents into the appropriate files, so they'll be there as notes when you come to work on each chapter.

Now that your book is laid out on your computer, print out a copy of your table of contents to keep beside you. This will be helpful as a reference while you write. The table of contents will change, of course. You may decide on new chapter names and revise headings and subheadings as you go along. As you finish each chapter, you'll add the headings to your table of contents and then print out a new copy. Sometimes it's helpful to place check marks next to the chapters or sections you've finished. You can also jot notes to yourself as a reminder to include this or that as ideas occur to you.

Before you start to write, there's one more file you should print out first—a copy of your original book proposal. Keep the file open on your hard drive as well. The proposal is going to provide you with the skeleton of your book. It's got the bare bones there already. Now you just have to add the meat.

Writing Your Book

Let's tackle your book one chunk at a time. Start with your original proposal. Go to the introduction or overview section of your proposal and copy it into the file for your book's introduction or first chapter. You probably won't be able to use all of the proposal's introduction in your book—the proposal addressed editors, and now you must address readers—but chances are you'll be able to use quite a bit of it. Go through it carefully, rewording where necessary.

You can work on it now or come back to it after you've written some of the other sections. Sometimes it's even easier to write the introduction after you've finished the book.

Next, go back to the proposal and copy the author bio section into your book's about-the-author file. You might want to modify it, but at least you've already written most of it.

If you're feeling a little nervous about starting the actual writing, you can tackle the appendices and some of the other back matter first: the bibliography, recommended reading list, resources, glossary of terms, and so on.

If in doubt about what the appendices should look like, turn to the back of this book or grab any nonfiction book from your own shelves and use that as a guide. Of course, if you have questions about anything along the way, give your editor a call. Writing a book that's under contract means you're not alone anymore. Your editor will most likely feel pleased to have input into the process, and it can mean fewer revisions for you later in the process.

Formatting Your Manuscript

Before you get too far into the writing of your book, it's a good idea to set up the manuscript format first. Create a directory on your computer to use specifically for this particular book. (You might have already done so when creating your query letter and proposal.) Open a new file for each chapter, including front matter and back matter.

> The most effective book introductions cover an aspect of the topic that doesn't get addressed in other sections of the book. The least effective introductions outline what the reader will encounter in the pages ahead. There's really no need for that. The book's table of contents tells readers what to expect.

Wise Words

Writing isn't hard. It isn't any harder than ditch-digging.

—Patrick Dennis

Follow these guidelines for formatting your book manuscript:

1. Include a cover page that has your name, address, phone number, and E-mail address in the upper left corner of the page. About halfway down the page and centered in the middle, type your book's title and your name.

    Do not number the title page or include the copyright symbol.

2. Double-space all remaining pages of your manuscript, including front matter and back matter.

3. Number your pages consecutively starting with the acknowledgments page or about-the-author page as page one.

4. On the top of every page of your manuscript have a running head that looks like this:

```
Your Last Name/Your Book Title              Page #
```

    Make sure your page numbers are on the right side of the page at the top. Your word processing program has a feature to make the header for you. Do not type a running head in on each page. Let the word processor place the header for you.

5. Use Times New Roman size 12 or Courier size 10 as your font.

6. You can use bold to indicate headings and chapter titles.

7. Start each new chapter on its own page. Type "Chapter 1" on the first line and center it. Type the name of the chapter just underneath and center that.

8. Start your text about a quarter of the way down the page.

Wise Words

Write a book that's as good as the proposal makes it sound.

—Dorian Karchmar

---

9. Allow for a one-inch to an inch-and-a-half margin all the way around the page.
10. Indent each paragraph five or six spaces.
11. Do not leave an extra space between paragraphs.

Organizing Your Thoughts

Once you've organized your research notes and set up your formatting, it's time to turn to the actual content for your book. How you present the material is very important. Paying attention to logical order will make your book flow evenly; neglecting logical order may mean turning in an unacceptable manuscript.

Logical order simply means what should come first, what should come after that, and so on. You've got a lot of thoughts and topics to cover. Write them all down. Then look for a thread, a logical way to present your thoughts. As an example, turn to the Contents for this book. There is a clear logical order for the presentation of material here. After the overview of the world of publishing, the book starts with finding ideas and proceeds to presenting those ideas to editors and agents, sealing a legal relationship when you sell the idea, researching and writing the book, and then taking promotional steps to sell the book to the actual readers. If this book's title (and purpose) happened to be *How to Write, Then Sell Your Nonfiction Book* instead of *How to Sell, Then Write Your Nonfiction Book*, the chapters would have to be arranged differently. Researching and writing would be covered before presenting, selling, and promoting it. Look for the logical order for your book's topic. And don't worry if you realize part of the way through that you need

---

Wise Words

Good writing is clear thinking made visible.

—Bill Wheeler

---

to switch a couple of chapters around. That can happen. Ideas crystallize as we work.

There must be a logical order within chapters, too. For this book it's logical to cover researching before getting down to writing. And in this chapter it makes sense to cover manuscript format before going on to writing style.

But it can get tricky—things aren't always clear-cut. For example, manuscript format could be covered either before or after writing the book. Some people write first, then worry about format when it's time to print out the manuscript. Others set up the proper format from the start. This book recommends setting up the format early on, but the section on formatting initially covered submitting the finished manuscript, too. Its heading was Formatting and Submitting the Manuscript. Because format should come before the book is written and submitting information should come afterward, it became necessary to divide the section into two parts, as you see here.

To help sort out the logical order for your book, grab a handful of index cards and write one chapter heading on each card. Then take another handful and write one subheading on each card. Spread them out on a large table or on the floor. Organize them logically. You can easily move them around from one chapter to another to see how things work best.

If you can't find an effective way to connect one thought to the next, create a new heading or subheading or consider moving the paragraph to a different section.

Transitions

To avoid jumping from one topic to the next, use connectors to make a smooth transition. Words such as *but, however, therefore,* and so on work as transitions. But drawing a parallel from the previous paragraph to the current one can be more effective. For example, the section on formatting manuscripts found earlier in this chapter starts with the sentence "Before you get too far into the writing of your book, it's a good idea to set up the manuscript format first." This connects to the section before it, which touches on writing the book, and also serves to connect to the sections that follow.

Unique Elements

Throughout this book you'll see elements that are set apart from the main text, including quotes and tips of the trade. How they are set apart and treated in relation to the main text is an editorial production and design decision. You can discuss your vision, but you won't have much control over it. You might indicate that special elements should be set apart as a sidebar, as boxed text, or with italics. Some sidebars or tips may be set in a deep margin; others may be set off by bold lines. Each house is unique and will have its own set of guidelines to work from and design to follow.

If you're unsure, discuss with your editor how he or she wants you to note the various elements in your manuscript. Some editors use square brackets around the words *Set as Sidebar* placed at the beginning of the sidebar and *End of Sidebar* at the end of the material you're asking to be set aside. Because each publishing house typically has its own preferred treatment for these types of issues, it's always in the best interest of your relationship with your editor to ask before you start writing.

Sidebars, quotes, and other special elements aren't necessary for every book, but sometimes they can add to it. These elements can help break up a lot of heavy and lengthy material. The material you'll place in a sidebar or boxed text could be related to the topic you're covering but would work well set off by itself. For example, if you're writing a travel book, you might include insider tips on each destination in each chapter—and those tips could be set off nicely in a sidebar.

In this book, related quotes and bits of advice are set apart from the body of the main text. They add visual appeal, are easy to read and digest, and break up the text in an interesting way.

Anecdotes, Case Studies, Quotes, and Interviews

If your book lends itself to anecdotes, case studies, quotes, or interviews, where should you put them? Some books start each chapter with a case study or anecdote. Others, like this one, start each chapter with a quote.

You can make the inclusion of a case study or anecdote work anywhere it will illustrate an important point you're making.

You can use quotes from experts as you go, placing them where they back up or add to what you're saying. Full-length interviews that cover a lot of ground can be placed anywhere in the chapter, as long as their positioning adheres to some sort of logical order. You can also break up a full-length interview to use bits and pieces where needed.

Feel free to edit the words the experts are giving you. You're expected to correct any grammar mistakes and to arrange the order in which the quotes are presented. But you're not expected to put words in an interviewee's mouth. Never change the intent of your contributor's words.

What if your expert or interview subject asks to see the finished chapter before you send it off to the publisher? Most writers decline. You're not giving your subjects editorial veto power. Assure all contributors that you will show them and their words in the best possible light—that all subjects end up looking good. If they insist, then you have a decision to make. If you're dealing with just one interviewee and that interview is crucial to your book, you don't have much bargaining room. But if you're interviewing quite a few people and you can easily substitute one for another, you can let your subjects know that.

When requesting an interview for print, make sure to explain exactly what you'll be doing. Will you use the person's name? Occupation? City? Business name? How much information will you reveal? Will you protect the person's privacy, if requested? Have your subjects send you a letter granting you permission to use their interviews in your book. Keep these on file in case your editor needs them to satisfy the publisher's legal department.

Writing Style

"I have a great deal of admiration for writers," says executive editor Kent Carroll of Carroll & Graf. "Good writing is a blessing, but it can be a difficult way to make a living. It can be frustrating and disappointing. There is no magical formula for success. You have to really love what you're doing. And if you really like it, you'll probably do it better."

Wise Words

The best way to become a successful writer is to read good writing, remember it, and then forget where you remember it from.

—Gene Fowler

It's true that when you're writing something that feels like drudgery, the result may sound like it, too. If it's something you feel passionate and energetic about, this will show in the words you use and how you structure your sentences. Always try to write what you love and it will show.

There are a few other things to consider, though, when writing your book—some of which may be dictated by your publisher. Is your editor expecting a formal style or an informal, chatty one?

Remember to match the style of writing you use for your book to the style you chose for your proposal. Know who your audience is and how your publisher prefers you address them. Will you use the informal second person? Will you include yourself in the book by using the first person? Or will you stick to the third person and avoid both? These are decisions with which your editor can help.

Whatever approach you ultimately decide to use, make it consistent throughout. Always strive for a readable book. "I want to read a piece of nonfiction with the same excitement I have when I read a novel," says agent Simon Lipskar (Writers House). So does everyone. Nonfiction readers want to be entertained as well as informed.

Writing Mistakes

It is said that there are two types of writers: those who can, and those who can't. (Not those who teach: those who teach usually can, too—they have to.) There's another category: those who can't but think they can.

Obviously, if you've gotten this far in the process, you're in the group who can. But all new writers can still make mistakes. "I wish writers would learn

Wise Words

If you ask someone, "Can you play the violin?" and he says, "I don't know, I've not tried, perhaps I can," you laugh at him. Whereas about writing, people always say, "I don't know, I have not tried," as though one had only to try and one would become a writer.

—Leo Tolstoy

the nuts and bolts of writing," says agent Frances Kuffel. "Learn grammar, punctuation. Learn that less is better." Make sure you master the basics—grammar, spelling, and punctuation—before sending material off to agents or editors. Although chronic bad English is a turnoff to editors, it's at least something that can be overcome by hard work. That level of writing can be taught. Cooperation and a good attitude usually can't (unless dealing with a child).

Every editor and agent has a horror story. Agent Jessica Faust (BookEnds) remembers, "Mine was while working with an author on a nonfiction book. One of the hardest things about working on nonfiction, more than fiction, is that the author is truly the expert. I don't know that much about bankruptcy taxes, physics, or speaking French, but I do know what makes a good book. This particular author refused to accept any of the editing changes I suggested and refused to help in the development of the book. Ultimately, she was a

Don't assume that your editor is there to correct your bad grammar. This is something you need to master yourself. He or she might clean up your first submission—there won't be any choice if the deadline is looming—but will remember the extra work you created when it comes time to assign or accept another book.

Wise Words

Like stones, words are laborious and unforgiving, and the
fitting of them together, like the fitting of stones,
demands great patience and strength of purpose and
particular skill.

—Edmund Morrison

---

prima donna. She simply wanted to write the book (which was a direct rehashing of a previous book) and have everyone tell her how wonderful it was. Unfortunately, the book ended up getting published as she wrote it and to scathing reviews. Your agent or editor doesn't know everything, but it is good to take into consideration those things she does know."

Submitting Your Manuscript

As you write, make sure to copy partial or finished chapters and other sections to a disk. Store the disk in a place other than your computer's hard drive. If your computer gets stolen or (heaven forbid) crashes, you want to make sure all your hard work doesn't disappear.

Most editors expect to receive a disk when you turn in the hard copy. Check with your editor that the word processing program you use is compatible with that used by the publisher.

Some contracts specify that two copies of the completed manuscript must be turned in. You can verify this with your editor.

When mailing in your completed manuscript and disk, be sure to include a brief cover letter. Note your name and the manuscript's title, and draw attention to the disk you've enclosed.

Send the pages loose or with an elastic band wrapped around them to hold them together. Editor Kent Carroll's feelings on the subject are representative of other editors: "I prefer manuscripts that are loose pages in a box rather than bound together. The easier it is to read, the cleaner it is, helps. It doesn't mean that somebody is going to like the book more. But when I get

a manuscript in small type or that is printed on one of those old ink-jet print-
ers that's difficult to see, I don't even want to look at it."

Your completed manuscript is now ready to be turned in. Does it feel as
if you've forgotten something? You haven't. For the first time during this
series of correspondence with editors and agents you've been conducting, you
do not need to include an SASE!

Meeting Deadlines

Your contract will specify when you must turn in your manuscript. This is
something you most likely discussed with your editor when talking about
your book's focus and contractual terms. Usually you'll receive anywhere
from six months to a year—and sometimes longer—to write and turn in
your book. It's always a good idea to get a head start and begin working on
your book before the deadline starts to loom.

Although some people work better with the pressure of a looming deadline, if you're a new writer and this is your first book, it's better to allow
plenty of leeway. What if you get sick (or someone in your family does)?
What if research material you had counted on doesn't pan out? What if someone who had promised an interview suddenly backs out? You want to have
plenty of time to deal with any contingencies.

If the unthinkable happens, though, and no matter how hard you try to
fix things, you realize you're going to be late, what do you do? Call your editor right away to let him or her know. If you give plenty of warning, there
might be enough time to reschedule the book's debut date. If you wait to the
last minute, your editor will be left high and dry. This won't endear you to
the publishing house—you can most likely forget about future book deals
coming your direction.

Page Proofs

Somewhere between the time you turn in your manuscript and its release
date, you'll most likely receive a set of galleys—or page proofs—in the mail
from your editor or the freelance copyeditor to whom your manuscript was
assigned. You'll be expected to go through the galleys and mark any mistakes. There also might be little Post-It notes querying items you've written.
You'll be expected to address each of those questions.

Make sure to use your spellchecker before printing out your manuscript and copying the files to disk. Some publishers typeset the book directly from the disk you provide. If you haven't caught all your mistakes, they might get missed on the editorial side as well.

Be careful going through the manuscript—check for misspelled names and that the table of contents and the page numbers match the chapter headings and page numbers within the manuscript. Be careful but not obsessive. Your galleys will also be checked by a professional proofreader. You're not expected to catch every typo.

Be sure to check the letter accompanying the page proofs and follow its directions. You might be given only a short period of time to review the manuscript and send it back. If it has arrived on your desk at an inopportune time, then call the project editor to extend the period of time you've been given.

When you're finished, check with your editor to see whether you need to turn in the entire set of galleys or only the pages for which you made corrections. (If you're responsible for the postage, the latter option can save you money.)

Staying Power

If your brain is starting to feel sluggish and the words aren't jumping onto the screen, don't assume right away that you've got a full-blown case of writer's block. You could be tired, and if that's the case, go take a nap or play a cou-

Wise Words

The cure for writer's cramp is writer's block.

—Inigo de Leon

ple of hands of solitaire. While you're resting, let your mind wander back to your material. Could be all you need to get jump-started is to work on another area of the book.

If you find yourself playing more solitaire than writing, though, you might need to force yourself to stick to it, so you can work through the feeling. Sometimes cleaning out all the information in a file (and saving it to a new file called Extra or Later), and starting with a clear screen will help clear your head. Make a list of what you want to cover. Even if it's just one little area, decide what must be said and in what order.

Another trick for beating a block is to start writing—anything. Let it be the opening lines to a novel you're contemplating or the lyrics to a favorite song as you hum them to yourself. Whatever gets your brain moving through your fingertips will work.

Here's one other thought to help motivate yourself to work through the brain strain. Once the book is done, you'll receive the second half of your advance. If that isn't enough, think about the finished product coming out with your name emblazoned on the cover. You can do this. As the opening quote of this chapter points out: "The art of writing is the art of applying the seat of the pants to the seat of the chair."

Wise Words

Writing is thinking on paper.

—William Zinsser

Selling Your Book to the Public

"If you want a place in the sun, you've got to expect a few blisters."
                                                                —Anonymous

ONCE YOUR BOOK is sold, written, and turned in to your publisher, you can start thinking about what you might do to help promote it. But isn't that the publisher's job? you might be wondering. In part, it is. Most large publishing houses have in-house promotion departments. They are equipped to create press kits, send out releases, and send authors on cross-country book signing tours. They're equipped to do it, but most will not—not unless they've earmarked your book as worthy of the big budget. In other words, unless your publisher has decided in advance—and told you about it—to get behind your book and spend the money necessary to make it a big seller (if not a bestseller), you can expect very little in the way of publisher-funded promotion. The same logically holds true for the midsize and smaller presses. For the average book that a publisher produces, you can expect a flyer for sales reps to show bookstores and libraries. Sometimes they'll send out a few review copies for you.

"Publishers may rely on the marketing and publicity efforts of authors to get the word out about their book," says Contemporary Books editor Denise Betts. "And there is a variety of ways for authors to do just that."

You don't have to feel miffed, though, if you think your publisher lacks enthusiasm when it comes to publicity. You can make your own. "Don't expect a publisher to promote your book," says PR consultant Pari Noskin Taichert. "It's up to you to create the initial enthusiasm about your work. You're your biggest fan—if you aren't, you've got a problem. I believe promotion is something we decide to do on a daily basis, whether we're aware of it or not. Every time we talk about a book we're reading, we're promoting it (or trashing it). So, why are writers so darn shy about talking about and selling their own work? There are hundreds of ways to promote your work, from generating word-of-mouth buzz to hiring a publicist. I'd suggest doing as many as a writer can think of and then—depending on funds—hiring someone else to do more."

Let's see in what activities a newly published author can participate:

1. Arrange your own speaking engagements and book signings.

   - Contact groups that would be interested in your book's topic and arrange to sell your book when you speak.
   - Contact bookstores in your area and let them know you're a local author with your first book coming out. Offer to speak on your book's topic.
   - Contact your local libraries and offer to speak at readers' group meetings.
   - Contact your local radio and television programs and offer to be interviewed.
   - Contact radio programs around the country. These interviews can be conducted via telephone. You don't even need to leave your house to appear on a national radio show.
   - Send review copies of your book to local newspaper book reviewers and other publications. (More on that later.)

2. Create a press kit.
3. Design a website.
4. Participate in related online chats.
5. Post notices about your book on related online bulletin boards.

Wise Words

Be entrepreneurial and tireless in helping promote your book after it's published.

—Dorian Karchmar

---

6. Run ads in newspapers or publications related to your book's topic.
7. Send direct mailings to friends and family via E-mail or regular postal service. (Don't be shy about selling the book to people you know—they might turn out to be your biggest fans.)
8. Arrange a private book signing party.

There are many ways to promote your book. Look for ways that are both enjoyable and effective.

The Anatomy of a Press Kit

The preceding list suggests you contact various outlets such as bookstores and radio shows. A press kit is the best way to make that contact. Public relations professional Gail Rubin (who is also author of *A Girl's Pocket Guide to Trouser Trout*, see Chapter 4) advises new writers to send their press kit to news media. "Be sure to send your press kit with a good pitch letter and a copy of the book; then make follow-up calls to arrange interviews for yourself."

The Encyclopedia of Associations is a good research tool to find related organizations. It includes nearly twenty-three thousand national and international organizations, with information on contacts, publications, meeting schedules with average attendance, and regional or local chapters. Most local libraries have a copy in their reference section.

> Speaking engagements often pull in more people than a book signing session. Offer your expertise to libraries and bookstores.

First, visit an office supply store and pick up several folders—the ones with pockets on either side and slits cut out to hold business cards work well. Make sure to use good-quality paper. "Don't use cheesy prefab stationery or computer-generated letterhead," says Gail Rubin. "It screams amateur! Your book is worth a good paper presentation."

Here's what a press kit package should include.

Outside the Folder

Pitch Letter You had to keep your query letter and proposal toned down as far as self-glorification was concerned. Your press kit is another matter; here you can be shamelessly promotional. Use the pitch line you prepared for your query, then go on to list the book's key points and the benefits it offers. Toot your horn here, too. Include all your related accomplishments.

A Copy of Your Book No one can review your book if you don't send it. Sometimes your publisher will send out review copies for you, if you send your editor a list. Other times you'll have to use up the supply of complimentary copies you were given or take advantage of the 50-percent-off deal your publisher extends for author copies. The postage might have to come out of your pocket, though.

Right Side of the Folder

The right side or right pocket of the folder is generally used for written presentations. Here you'll include:

Press Release The press release contains the who, what, when, where, and how much—snappy info about your book and why someone would want to read it. You hope a publication will print your press release as is. Be sure to make it easy for editors to do that. Give all the important facts right up front. Don't make anyone dig through excess verbiage to get to the heart of your book's topic and its appeal. Make sure to include your contact information. If your press release is successful, someone will want to get in touch for an interview or speaking engagement.

Author Q&A Again, you want to make it as easy as possible for would-be interviewers. If you present them with a list of questions, they'll know exactly what to ask you—and you'll know how to answer those questions, since you thought them up yourself. Approach the exercise as though you were interviewing another author. What would you ask? Then translate those questions to fit the interesting and compelling aspects of your book. (Some busy interviewers never get a chance to read the book, so they can't figure out what to ask. Your list of questions will help save them time and energy, and they'll appreciate that.)

Fact Sheet Book fact sheets include information such as the number of pages, book dimensions, the price of the book, the publisher, the ISBN (International Standard Book Number), and ordering/purchasing information.

Book Excerpts Look for short passages from your book that grab attention and interest. Include them in your press release or on a separate sheet of paper.

Quotes Include quotes from any advance book reviews or jacket blurbs. Has anyone endorsed your book? Include those quotes, too.

Left Side of the Folder

Use the left side of the folders for graphics or artwork such as:

Author Photo and Biography Have a good photo of yourself taken. Use a professional; you don't want to skimp on quality. You can print your author biography on the back of the photo or make up a two-page spread.

Book Cover Art Include a book jacket or color copy of the jacket or cover. Sometimes you can get extra jackets from your publisher. If not, take one to any copy center and make color copies.

Other Material You can also include copies of press clippings, book reviews, and any articles related to your topic. Some authors have book markers or postcards made up with the book's title or cover art on them. Make your press kit attractive, tidy, and easy to navigate.

What to Send to the Media and When

Make a list of appropriate publications (references are provided in Appendix B) and send them material following this schedule.

Six Months to Two Years Prior to Publication

Long-Lead and Specialty Magazines Some magazines require you to send material far in advance. To these magazines you can send:

- **Book excerpts.** Make sure to attach permission to reprint. Specify that excerpts can be printed as long as you are given credit and your book's title is mentioned.
- **Review copies of your book.** Magazine book review editors need a long lead-in time because they receive a lot of books to review. In some cases, you can send publisher's galleys or page proofs if your book hasn't come out yet. Check with the reviewer's office to make sure that's acceptable.

At Least Two Months Prior to Publication

Book Trade Publications Send galleys or page proofs to *Publishers Weekly* and others. Ask your editor for more leads.

Newspapers/Magazines

- Book review sections (review copies of your book)
- Feature sections (articles, your press kit, author Q&A)

- Editorial opinions (letters to the editor)
- Columnists (articles, your press kit, author Q&A)
- Local angles to story (your press kit with a sheet specifying the local angle)

Television/Radio

- Pitch yourself and your book to radio talk show interviewers.
- Offer yourself as an expert resource for reporters and producers.
- Arrange book tour tie-ins. Let news media know when you'll be in town to do book signings.

Should You Hire a Publicist?

Publicists can be expensive, but they may be able to get the job done for you more quickly and effectively than you can do it yourself. Be realistic about the sales you can expect from the book. Will these sales ultimately pay back your advance and also justify the cost of a publicist? If so, then go for it.

Public relations consultant Pari Noskin Taichert says, "I'd hire a publicist in a minute to get book signings for myself and to come up with ways to get the word out about my book. A good publicist will generate more ideas than straight publicity and will be public relations–focused rather than just getting freebies."

The Cost of Publicity

Publicists schedule their fees in different ways. Some might charge by the hour; some might charge an up-front monthly retainer. Others will quote a flat rate and charge by the project. Hourly rates can run from $25 to $125 and up.

Public relations professional Gail Rubin says, "I'd estimate a minimum fee of $500, plus expenses for postage, long-distance calls, and supplies. A full book promotion by a publicist could likely cost more than several thousand dollars."

"There are things writers need to understand before they work with a publicist," explains Pari Noskin Taichert. "For example, they don't own this person's time—only a small portion of it. Unless you can hire a publicist full-time, he or she will have other clients making demands as well. Personally, I'd prefer to pay a publicist a retainer or by the hour rather than by the project."

Wise Words

The best thing you can do about critics is never say a word. In the end you have the last say, and they know it.

—Tennessee Williams

When the Reviews Are Bad

When your PR efforts start to pay off, you might begin seeing some reviews of your book. Your editor will most likely send you copies of any he or she runs across. It's exciting to see what someone else has to say about your book. Exciting—and scary, too. What if they don't like your book?

There's an old saying that bad press is better than no press. And it's true. There's nothing you can do about it except toughen up your skin.

Humorist Fran Lebowitz offers a helpful perspective on the issue: "Certainly America is not overrun by great literary critics. The way I feel about reviews: My career has really been made by them, because I have gotten mostly good reviews. I am always happy to get good reviews because I want people to buy my books. But by and large, with some exceptions, your good reviews are usually as stupid as your bad reviews."

Cautions

Here are some words of advice from the professionals:

Executive Editor Kent Carroll

"One of the things that has become apparent to writers is that when they get published, they can do a lot to promote their own books and help sell them. The more attention a book gets, the better it sells. But some overdo it. I think some writers read in a magazine somewhere that if you pester your publisher enough, they will do all of these things for you. Not true.

"If you pester your publisher enough, they may stop doing anything for you. Your publisher is not your adversary. The both of you should work together because you have the same purpose in mind; that is, to publish the book as well as you can and to sell as many copies as possible.

"Work to do what you can in conjunction with the publisher. Let them know what you are doing so there's some mutuality in it. The author who demands things or is unreasonable or unrealistic is not doing himself or herself any favor."

PR Professional Gail Rubin

"Don't send materials out blindly. Call to make sure the person to whom you are planning to send your book is still working there and would be the appropriate recipient."

PR Professional Pari Noskin Taichert

"Don't fall into the trap of thinking that publicity is the main way to fame and fortune. Getting a blurb in the paper or on the news is fleeting. Selling is much more about word of mouth and person-to-person relationships."

Selling the Next Book and the Book After That

You've just finished your first book; isn't it too soon to be thinking about the next one? It's never too soon. In fact, you could start making plans for the second book around the time you're proposing the first. Remember all that research you did with publisher catalogs and *Books in Print?* You probably gleaned some useful ideas there. Did you find a series you could contribute to or other holes in publishers' lists?

Of course, you've been cultivating a pleasant working relationship with your editor, and during conversations you might have mentioned doing another book for that publishing house. If not, it's not too late to get on the phone and ask for hints, suggestions, or leads for your next project.

If you acquired an agent in this process, make sure to check in with him or her. Editors often let agents know when they're looking for books covering particular topics. Your agent might have the perfect lead for you.

The most important thing to remember about this process is you are not the same person you were when you started proposing your first book. You are now possibly agented. And you are definitely a published author. You have credits! Use those credits to your advantage as you write the author bio section of your next query letter and proposal.

APPENDIX A:

Resources

MOST PROFESSIONAL ASSOCIATIONS provide information on how to write and get published. Several offer job-location services for freelancers. A letter, an E-mail, or a visit to a website can put you in contact with a wealth of leads in your areas of interest.

The following is a sampling of key associations. When available, websites are noted.

Domestic Associations for Writers

American Association for the
Advancement of Science (AAAS)
1200 New York Ave., N.W.
Washington, DC 20005
rnichols@aaas.org
www.aaas.org

American Medical Writers' Association
(AMWA)
9650 Rockville Pike
Bethesda, MD 20814
amwa@amwa.org
www.amwa.org

American Society of Journalists and
Authors (ASJA)
1501 Broadway, Suite 302
New York, NY 10036
www.asja.org

American Translators Association (ATA)
1800 Diagonal Rd., Suite 220
Alexandria, VA 22314
www.atanet.org

Association for Business Communication
(ABC)
Box G-1326, Baruch College
17 Lexington Ave.
New York, NY 10010
myersabc@compuserve.com
www.theabc.org

Association for Computing Machinery's
Special Interest Group on
Documentation (ACM/SIGDOC)
1515 Broadway, 17th Floor
New York, NY 10036
www.acm.org/sigdoc

Association for Educational
Communications and Technology
1025 Vermont Ave., N.W., Suite 820
Washington, DC 20005
www.aect.org

Association for Women in
Communications (AWC)
780 Ritchie Highway, Suite 28-S
Severna Park, MD 21146
www.womcom.org

Association of Teachers of Technical
Writing (ATTW)
Department of Rhetoric and
Writing Studies
San Diego State University
San Diego, CA 92182-4452
www.rhet.agri.umn.edu/~tcq

Authors Guild
31 E. Twenty-eighth St., 10th Floor
New York, NY 10016
www.authorsguild.org

Copywriter's Council of America
Communications Building
102 Seven Putter Ln.
Middle Island, NY 11953

Council for Programs in Technical and
Scientific Communication (CPTSC)
New Mexico State University
English Department, Box 3E
Las Cruces, NM 88003

Council for the Advancement of Science
Writing
Abbotts Building, Room 100
Philadelphia, PA 19104

Council of Biology Editors (CBE)
60 Revere Dr., #500
Northbrook, IL 60062

Editorial Freelancers Association (EFA)
71 W. Twenty-third St.
New York, NY 10010

Education Writers Association
1331 H St., N.W., #307
Washington, DC 20005
www.ewa.org

Fiction Writer's Connection (FWC)
(directed by Blythe Camenson)
bcamenson@aol.com
www.fictionwriters.com

Freelance Editorial Association
P.O. Box 835
Cambridge, MA 02238

Health Sciences Communications
Association
6728 Old McLean Village Dr.
McLean, VA 22101

IEEE Professional Communication
Group
345 E. Forty-seventh St.
New York, NY 10017

Institute of Electrical and Electronics
Engineers' Professional Communication
Society (IEEE/PCS)
IEEE Operations Center, Admission and
Advancement Department
445 Hoes Ln., P.O. Box 459
Piscataway, NJ 08855-0459
www.ieee.org/society/pcs

National Association of Agricultural
Journalists
c/o Audrey Mackiewitz
312 Valley View Dr.
Huron, OH 44839

National Association of Black Journalists
P.O. Box 17212
Washington, DC 20041

National Association of Government
Communicators
609 S. Washington St.
Alexandria, VA 22314
www.nagc.com

National Association of Hispanic
Journalists
National Press Building
Washington, DC 20045

National Association of Science Writers
P.O. Box 294
Greenlawn, NY 11740
www.nasw.org

National Conference of Editorial Writers
6223 Executive Blvd.
Rockville, MD 20852

National Federation of Press Women
Box 99
Blue Springs, MO 64013

National Writers Union (NWU)
National Office East
113 University Pl., 6th Floor
New York, NY 10003
nwu@nwu.org
www.nwu.org

National Writers Union (NWU)
National Office West
337 Seventeenth St., #101
Oakland, CA 94612
(Job Hotline) hotline@nwu.org
(regular E-mail) nwu@nwu.org
www.nwu.org

Science Fiction Writers of America
Five Winding Brook Dr., #18
Guilderland, NY 12084
www.sfwa.org

Society for Technical
Communication, Inc.
901 N. Stuart St., Suite 904
Arlington, VA 22203
www.stc-va.org

Society of American Travel Writers
1155 Connecticut Ave., Suite 500
Washington, DC 20006

Writers Guild of America (WGA) East
555 W. Fifty-seventh St.
New York, NY 10019
www.wgaeast.org

Writers Guild of America (WGA) West
7000 W. Third St.
Los Angeles, CA 90048
www.wga.org

Canadian Associations for Writers

Association of Canadian Publishers
110 Eglinton Ave., W., Suite 401
Toronto, Ontario M4R 1A3
Canada
www.publishers.ca

Canadian Authors Association
275 Slater St., Suite 500
Ottawa, Ontario K1P 5H9
Canada

Canadian Magazine Publishers
Association
130 Spadina Ave., Suite 202
Toronto, Ontario M5V 2L4
Canada
www.cmpa.ca

Canadian Publishers' Council
250 Merton St., Suite 203
Toronto, Ontario M4S 1B1
Canada
www.pubcouncil.ca

Societe Quebecoise de la Redaction
Professionelle (SQRP)
C.P. 126
Succursale Roxboro
Roxboro, Quebec H8Y 3ES
Canada
christop@total.net

Writers Union of Canada
24 Ryerson Ave.
Toronto, Ontario M5R 2G3
Canada

International Associations for Writers

Australia Society for Technical
Communication (ASTC)
68 Holmes Rd.
Moonee Ponds
Victoria, Australia 3039
Contact: Julie Fisher
www.vicnet.net.au/~astc

Gesellschaft fuer Technische
Kommunikation (TEKOM)
Markelstrasse 34
D-70193 Stuttgart
Germany
www.tekom.de

Gesellschaft fuer Technische
Kommunikation Schweiz
(TECOM Schweiz)
Kirchbergstrasse 30
CH-5024 Kuttigen
Switzerland
www.tecom.ch

Institute of Scientific and Technical
Communicators (ISTC)
Blackhorse Rd.
Letchworth, Hertfordshire SG6 1YY
England
www.istc.org.uk

International Association of Audiovisual
Communicators (IAAVC)
9531 Jamacha Blvd., #263
Spring Valley, CA 91977
www.cindys.com

International Association of Business
Communicators (IABC)
One Hallidie Plaza, #600
San Francisco, CA 94102
www.iabc.com

International Communication
Association (ICA)
Box 9589
Austin, TX 78766-9589
icahdq@uts.cc.utexas.edu

International Council for Technical
Communication
106 South Airmont Rd.
Suffern, NY 10901-7731
www.nts.mh.se/~fti/intecom.htm

International Interactive
Communications Society (IICS)
10160 S.W. Nimbus Ave., Suite F2
Portland, OR 97223
www.iics.org

International Society for Performance
Improvement (ISPI)
1300 L St., N.W., Suite 1250
Washington, DC 20005
www.ispi.org

International Television and Video
Association (ITVA)
6311 N. O'Connor Rd., Suite 230
Irving, TX 75039
www.itva.org

Book Publishing

American Booksellers Association
Information Service Center
828 S. Broadway
Tarrytown, NY 10591
info@bookweb.org
www.ambook.org

American Society of Business Publication
Editors
710 E. Ogden Ave., Suite 600
Naperville, IL 60563
www.asbpe.org

Association of American Publishers
(AAP)
50 F St., N.W., 4th Floor
Washington, DC 20001
www.publishers.org

Association of American University
Presses (AAUP)
71 W. Twenty-third St., Suite 901
New York, NY 10010
www.aaupnet.org

Association of Authors'
Representatives (AAR)
P.O. Box 237201, Ansonia Station
New York, NY 10003
www.publishersweekly.com/aar

Audio Publishers Association
627 Aviation Way
Manhattan Beach, CA 90266
www.audiopub.org

Electronic Publishing Coalition
P.O. Box 35
Ellsworth, ME 04605
www.epccentral.org/members.html

National Association of Independent
Publishers
P.O. Box 430
Highland City, FL 33846-0430
naip@aol.com
www.publishersreport.com

Publishers Marketing Association
627 Aviation Way
Manhattan Beach, CA 90266
www.pma-online.org

Publishers Weekly
245 W. Seventeenth St., 6th Floor
New York, NY 10011
www.publishersweekly.com

Small Publishers Association of North
America (SPAN)
P.O. Box 1306
425 Cedar St.
Buena Vista, CO 81211
www.spannet.org

Promotion

American Advertising Federation
1101 Vermont Ave., N.W., Suite 500
Washington, DC 20005-6306
www.aaf.org

Meeting Professionals International
(MPI)
4455 LBJ Freeway, Suite 1200
Dallas, TX 75244-5903
www.mpiweb.org

Point of Purchase Advertising Institute
1600 L St., N.W., 10th Floor
Washington, DC 20036
www.popai.com

Public Relations Society of America
33 Irving Pl.
New York, NY 10003-2376
www.prsa.org

Magazines

Council of Literary Magazines and
Presses
clmpnyc@aol.com
www.litline.org

Magazine Publishers of America
919 Third Ave.
New York, NY 10022
www.magazine.org

Society of National Association
Publications
1595 Spring Hill Rd., Suite 330
Vienna, VA 22182
www.snaponline.org

Newspapers and Newsletters

American Society of Media
Photographers
150 N. Second St.
Philadelphia, PA 19106
www.asmp.org

American Society of Newspaper Editors
P.O. Box 4090
Reston, VA 22090-1700
www.asne.org

Dow Jones Newspaper Fund
P.O. Box 300
Princeton, NJ 08543-0300
www.dowjones.com

International Newspaper Marketing
Association (INMA)
10300 N. Central Expressway, Suite 467
Dallas, TX 75231
www.inma.org

National Press Photographers Association
(NPPA)
3200 Cloasdaile Dr., Suite 306
Durham, NC 27705
www.nppa.org

Newsletter & Electronic Publishers
Association
1501 Wilson Blvd., Suite 509
Arlington, VA 22209
www.newsletters.org

Newspaper Association of America
1921 Gallows Rd., Suite 600
Vienna, VA 22182
www.naa.org

Newspaper Guild
501 Third St., N.W., Suite 250
Washington, DC 20001
www.newsguild.org

Tidbits (the online newsletter of the
Fiction Writer's Connection)
www.fictionwriters.com

APPENDIX B:

References

Market Guides

Market guides are invaluable for finding literary agents and publishing houses. They list agents' and editors' names and what they represent or publish. Many provide information on how these agents and editors want to be approached. Most come out annually. Because things change rapidly from year to year, sometimes even before a new guide has come to print, always use the most current guide and double-check its information. The editor you want to query may have moved to another department or another house, or the agent who didn't charge fees last year does now. Always send for guidelines with an SASE.

Guide to Literary Agents. Published annually by Writer's Digest Books, this guide distinguishes between agents who charge fees and those who don't and notes Association of Authors' Representatives (AAR) affiliation next to the names of member agents. It also lists the subject areas the agents handle, with information on how they prefer to be approached.

The International Directory of Little Magazines and Small Presses. This is published by Dustbooks each year and is a good reference when you're looking for houses for your nonfiction book.

Literary Market Place (LMP). This annual guide, published by R. R. Bowker, is priced too high for most new writers' budgets, but it is available in the reference section of any public library. It has the most comprehensive listing of publishers and agents, but the information provided for each listing is sketchy.

Novel & Short Story Writer's Market. Published by Writer's Digest Books, this guide is perfect for fiction writers. It also contains many articles. (Writer's Digest Books also publishes separate books for individual genres in fiction.)

Writer's Guide to Book Editors, Publishers, and Literary Agents, 2002–2003: Who They Are! What They Want! And How to Win Them Over! Agent Jeff Herman's annual guide gives brief histories of editors and book publishers and also indicates which editors work with which genres. He doesn't list many agents but offers more details on them than the other guides.

The Writer's Handbook. Published once a year by *The Writer* magazine, this book includes more articles but fewer listings than *Writer's Market.*

Writer's Market. Published annually by Writer's Digest Books, this guide lists more than eight thousand editors but only seventy-five or so agents. It's helpful for nonfiction writers. In addition to publisher listings, each year's *Writer's Market* contains articles on various aspects of writing and getting published. This is a must-have for any writer who wants to be published.

Periodicals

Library resources for researching newspapers, magazines, and broadcast outlets include the following:

Gale Directory of Publications & Broadcast Media. This publication provides contacts for television and radio stations across the United States organized by regions. It includes indexes for publishers, magazines, religious publications, radio stations and formats, paid community papers, and regional directories, as well as maps for top markets. A pricey volume, it weighs in at $800 plus. Used copies are available through Amazon.com at around $200 plus. Visit your local library to use it for free.

Publishers Weekly. The industry standard, this is a great resource for writers. It provides current market, bestseller, and trend information. Subscription information is available online at publishersweekly.com or by mail from 245 W. 17th St., 6th Floor, New York, NY 10011.

Small Press Review. This monthly, put out by the publisher of *The International Directory of Little Magazines and Small Presses,* offers reviews and updates on small and independent publishers. You can subscribe by writing to Dustbooks, Box 100, Paradise, CA 95967.

The Standard Periodical Directory. This comprehensive directory provides information on more than seventy-five thousand U.S. and Canadian periodicals—newspapers, news magazines, newsletters, and trade publications—in more than 250 categories. You can find more information at mediafinder.com.

Tidbits. A free online newsletter put out by author Blythe Camenson, this lists events, member success stories, and scams to watch out for. It is helpful for nonfiction and fiction writers. Free to members of Fiction Writer's Connection, it is available at fictionwriters.com or via E-mail to bcamenson@aol.com.

Ulrich's Periodicals Directory. Volume 5 of this annual publication features U.S. newspapers, both daily and weekly, by market. To order, visit ulrichsweb.com.

The Writer. This monthly magazine contains how-to articles, interviews, and other useful information. More information is available from *The Writer,* 120 Boylston St., Boston, MA 02116-4615.

Writer's Digest. This is the most well-known and helpful magazine on the market. Published monthly, it offers writers market updates, inspirational how-to articles, contests, profiles of successful writers, and more. The magazine is part of the company that publishes books under three imprints, including Writer's Digest Books, and runs its own book club for writers. For more information, write to *Writer's Digest,* 1507 Dana Ave., Cincinnati, OH 45207 or call 800-289-0963.

Writer's News. A friendly, chatty monthly market update, *Writer's News* mixes market updates, writing tips, and quotes. The personality of its editor, Elizabeth Klungness, comes through on every page. For subscription information write to Tower Enterprises, 2130 Sunset Dr. #47, Vista, CA 92083-4516 or call 760-941-9293.

Books

Career Portraits: Writing by Blythe Camenson (Contemporary Books). For young writers in middle school or higher, this publication addresses many aspects of writing and provides firsthand accounts from working writers.

Careers in Publishing by Blythe Camenson (Contemporary Books). Careers in book publishing, production, and publishing law; careers for writers, illustrators, and photographers; and how to become a literary agent or editor are all discussed here.

Careers in Writing by Blythe Camenson (Contemporary Books). For anyone wanting to explore a career in writing, this book covers nonfiction, fiction, freelance writing, staff writing and reporting, screenwriting, technical writing, marketing, advertising and public relations writing, and more.

Writing Creative Nonfiction edited by Carolyn Forche and Philip Gerard (Story Press). Instructions and insights from the teachers of the Associated Writing Programs are provided, as is a series of articles covering the art, craft, and business of writing creative nonfiction.

Your Novel Proposal: From Creation to Contract: The Complete Guide to Writing Query Letters, Synopses and Proposals for Agents and Editors by Blythe Camenson and Marshall J. Cook (Writer's Digest Books). The counterpart to *How to Sell, Then Write Your Nonfiction Book*, this guide teaches fiction writers how to approach editors and agents with their novels.

About the Author

BLYTHE CAMENSON is a full-time writer with more than four dozen books and numerous articles to her credit. Her books cover careers, writing, and getting published. She is coauthor of *Your Novel Proposal: From Creation to Contract* (Writer's Digest Books) and the author of *Careers in Writing* (Contemporary Books).

As director of the Fiction Writer's Connection (FWC), a membership organization for new writers, she teaches members how to improve their writing and how to get published. She offers E-mail courses in query letter and book proposal writing and provides free consultation and critiques to members. She works with both fiction and nonfiction writers. Visit her website at fictionwriters.com or contact her at bcamenson@aol.com.